HOW TO READ AND WRITE ABOUT FICTION

DR. WILLIAM KENNEY

Manhattan College

ARCO
New York

Second Edition

Copyright © 1988 by William Kenney

First Edition copyright © 1966 by Simon & Schuster

 ARCO

Simon & Schuster, Inc.
Gulf + Western Building
One Gulf + Western Plaza
New York, NY 10023

DISTRIBUTED BY PRENTICE HALL TRADE

Manufactured in the United States of America

1 2 3 4 5 6 7 8 9 10

Library of Congress Cataloging-in-Publication Data

Kenney, W. P. (William Patrick), 1933–
   How to read and write about fiction / by William Kenney. —2nd ed.
   p. cm.
   Rev. ed. of: How to analyze fiction. © 1966.
   Bibliography: p.
   Includes index.
   ISBN 0-13-431164-7 : $6.95
   1. Fiction—Technique.   2. Fiction—History and criticism.
I. Kenney, W. P. (William Patrick), 1933– How to analyze fiction.
II. Title.
PN3355.K45 1988
808.3—dc19   88-14157
              CIP

CONTENTS

INTRODUCTION
FICTION AND THE READER

Stories exist to be read. In fact, we might even say that a story doesn't exist—doesn't fully exist, anyway—except as it's being read. The words on a page are just that—words or, more accurately, shapes on a page—until the reader, in processing them, turns them into a story. And this means that reading is an activity, not a passivity. You the reader have a job to do: the job of bringing a story to life, constructing its meaning and realizing its form.

To do this job you need the appropriate equipment. Essentially, you're required to bring to the act of reading your worldly knowledge and your critical competence.

Your worldly knowledge is everything you think you know about the world and the people in it, including how those people do behave and how they should behave. I say "everything you think you *know*" because what I'm talking about isn't just some casual opinion you picked up yesterday and will drop later this afternoon but your more abiding and deeply held notions about the world you live in. I say "everything you *think* you know" because, as we all realize on reflection, some of our more abiding and deeply held notions are simply wrong; others are at best partly right. In fact, in your lifetime, you've no doubt already changed your mind, perhaps more than once, about the world and the people in it.

At any rate, insofar as stories are about the world—and all stories are, even those that are supposedly set in some other world—they carry with them their own burden of worldly knowledge, which may or may not correspond in all respects to yours. To a great extent, of course, a story's worldly knowledge remains implicit. That is, what the story tells us about these particular characters doing these particular things in this particular situation seems to imply something about the world at large: for instance, that this is truly how people do or would or should behave in a situation like this. Part of the reader's job is precisely to pick up those implications.

As I've said, the worldly knowledge of the story may more or less correspond to your own. But what if it doesn't? Well, let's consider the circumstances in which this situation may arise.

One possibility is that the story was written in a time or place (or both) distant from your own. For the truth is that worldly knowledge doesn't stand still. There are things you and I take for granted as Americans of this particular period that are very different even from what our grandparents took for granted. That's one reason we try not to forget that our worldly knowledge is what we *think* we know. We should be prepared, then, to find differences between our worldly knowledge and that implied by stories from other times and places.

Now when this happens, our first reaction may be to find the implications of the story strange and foreign or to congratulate ourselves on knowing how things *really* are. But we do at least recognize that our worldly knowledge is not and has never been shared by everybody, and that seems to be something worth knowing.

It's worth knowing because it allows us to place our worldly knowledge in a new perspective. Yes, we learn something from such an experience about, say, how people used to think, but don't we also learn something about how *we* think? For, after all, since we recognize that our worldly knowledge is only what we think we know, we can't take for granted that being born in our time and place means that in any particular area our worldly knowledge is sounder than that implicit in the text. At any rate, we may dramatically recognize in such an experience that our worldly knowledge is precisely that—ours. And that's a salutary experience.

A truly dizzying experience can arise out of this. I've suggested that our first reaction is to judge the story's worldly knowledge by measuring it against the standard of our own. But if we let it, the process may reverse itself. That is, we may provisionally accept the story's worldly knowledge as the standard—and realize the delightfully vertiginous experience of seeing the world and the people in it, which we've been taking for granted, suddenly appear to us as strange and foreign.

The recognition that the story's worldly knowledge is not in all respects your own isn't limited to stories from distant times and places. It may also happen when you read a contemporary American writer— say, Ann Beattie, Raymond Carver, William Gaddis, Toni Morrison— and find that that writer's America is very different from your own. This can be more disturbing because you can't say, "Times have changed," and shrug your shoulders. But again, at least you learn something about the worldly knowledge of your contemporaries, including wherein it differs from yours, and you also learn thereby something about your own worldly knowledge.

Reading fiction, then, involves a constant interaction between your worldly knowledge and that of the story. When the worldly knowledge of the story differs from your own, you do not therefore reject the story. You rather accept the opportunity to inform yourself of how the world looks from a perspective other than your own, and it's even possible that the story may lead you to revise your worldly knowledge in some respect.

We should realize that the process we're talking about is a dynamic one. It's going on constantly as we read, in fact it is in a sense *how* we read and construct the meaning of the story.

But in addition to worldly knowledge, we need to bring to the job of reading what we've called critical competence. It may be, for example, that if a character in a story acts in a way inconsistent with your worldly knowledge, the explanation is that the character's behavior is determined by literary convention. If, for example, a murder has been committed by implausibly complicated means under improbably unlikely circumstances, the explanation may not have much to do with worldly knowledge. It may be that you're reading a formal detective story, and that is the sort of thing that happens, by convention, in formal detective stories. But, of course, you can't understand that if you don't know the convention. Knowing the conventions, strategies, forms, and genres of literature, specifically of fiction, is what in this case we mean by critical competence.

Reading fiction, then, is a matter of addressing the text—and permitting it to address you—in the light of your worldly knowledge and critical competence. This book will not do anything directly for your worldly knowledge. Its more modest aim is to contribute to your critical competence by examining some of the elements of fiction and giving some attention to how these elements combine to produce a coherent whole that is meaningful and valuable.

In choosing examples, I have been guided largely by two considerations: literary merit and availability. If I have weighted the discussion to some extent in favor of the established rather than the new, that is in part because these texts have proven their staying power—not exactly a criterion of excellence but perhaps an indication of it. Also, there is some degree of critical consensus about these texts; choices among contemporary writers are inevitably more idiosyncratic. Finally, the novels I mention are, as I write these words, all in print, most of them in paperback editions, and the short stories are widely anthologized. The reader is encouraged, of course, to read as many of these texts as possible and to test what is said in this book against what the works of fiction tell you about themselves.

I felt it might be desirable to approach one text from a number of different angles, to avoid the suggestion that each story is responsive to only one or to a limited number of critical approaches. For this purpose I chose Nathaniel Hawthorne's "Young Goodman Brown." The story has been included as an appendix to this book.

One point of clarification: the word "story" as I use it is synonymous with "work of fiction" and may apply either to a short story or to a novel.

CHAPTER ONE
NARRATIVE STRUCTURE

CHOICE

FICTION AND CHOICE: The act of writing, whether one is writing a three-volume novel or a personal letter, consists of a series of choices. To see just what this means, let's consider the simpler form, the personal letter, first.

CHOICE IN A PERSONAL LETTER: In writing a personal letter, we begin making choices at the very beginning—at the salutation, as it is usually called. We begin "Dear ——." Dear what? Analyzing our relationship to the intended recipient of the letter permits us to choose the salutation properly. If the letter is to a personal friend, we probably use our friend's first name, perhaps even a nickname. A more distant acquaintance calls for a more formal salutation; a closer acquaintance may suggest a more intimate salutation—on the one hand, "Dear Mr. Brown"; on the other hand, "Darling." The choice is ours.

Of course, the choice is not entirely free. We are limited to some extent by custom, to some extent by what we suppose to be the expectations of the person who is to read the letter. Still, we must decide what custom applies to the situation in which we find ourselves. We must decide to what extent we are prepared in this set of circumstances to be bound by custom. We must decide just what are the expectations of the person to whom we address ourselves. And we may have to decide whether there is some good reason to disappoint those expectations. For instance, she may expect me to address her as "Darling," because that is what I usually do, but I want her to know at once that I'm displeased with her: "Dear Mary."

Many of the choices we make in such situations are not, of course, conscious choices in the strongest sense of that term. Most of the time we instinctively choose the right salutation and make similarly correct choices right down to the closing ("Sincerely"? "Love"?). But conscious or not, all of them are significant. All of them contribute to the total meaning we communicate to the reader.

CHOICE IN WRITING A STORY: The writer of fiction, like the writer of a letter, faces a series of choices. Some of the writer's choices are fully conscious; some are not. But all are significant; all contribute to making the story what it is and not something else.

Further, the writer of fiction, again like the writer of a letter, must make choices from a range of options that, though wide, is not infinite. Conventions, in some cases established by the practice of writers over many centuries, have led to the development of expectations on the part of readers. The writer must take these conventions and expectations into account. But it is finally the writer who must decide which conventions are appropriate to what he or she is doing. The writer must decide whether in this case to follow or to depart from convention. The writer must decide which of the reader's expectations are relevant to this particular story. And the writer may decide to violate the reader's expectations for the sake of some higher purpose.

CHOICE AND THE READER: What have the choices facing the writer of fiction to do with the experience of the reader of fiction? I suggest that the best way of developing an awareness of what's going on in any story you may read is to develop an awareness of the choices the author has made, the choices that give the story its distinctive shape. This includes, of course, some awareness of the alternatives open to the author, the kind of awareness a book like this is designed to help you develop. Your purpose is not to determine why the author made these choices (indeed, the author may not be sure) but rather to discover how the author's choices have combined to produce the unified story you have before you.

THE CHOICE OF SUBJECT: It is natural to think of the writer's series of choices as beginning with the choice of subject. In fact, however, the writer may not begin by thinking in terms of subject at all. A chance remark, a fleeting insight into character, a striking image—any of these may be the origin of a story. Such matters are, however, more relevant to the writer's biography or to the study of the creative process than to the analysis of a particular story. If the writer does not always begin with a subject, the reader is inclined to begin by wondering what the story is about—which is one way of saying what the subject is. And this is surely a question (again, perhaps not consciously asked) that the writer must, at least implicitly, answer early in the process of writing the story.

SUBJECT

THE MEANING OF SUBJECT: But of course the writer, unlike the reader, does not merely discover the subject; the writer chooses it, although the choice may be so instinctively made as to seem almost a discovery. Words like *subject, content, form,* and *style* are so freely and frequently used in discussions of literature that we must try always to be sure of what we mean by them. Often *subject* and *content* are treated as synonyms. In this book they are not. *Content*, as I use the term, means what the work contains. Content is essentially identical with form. We may sometimes find it desirable, for purposes of discussion, to act as though there were a distinction between the two, but we should do this as seldom as possible (for it's a bad habit to get into), and we should always remain aware that the distinction is even more artificial than most critical distinctions.

Subject, on the other hand, is not what the work contains but what the work may be said to refer to. Unlike the content, the subject exists before the story is written and would exist if the story were never written. For instance, we might consider the problems of a certain kind of middle-class woman in nineteenth-century France to be the subject of Gustave Flaubert's famous novel *Madame Bovary* (I don't suggest this is the only possible formulation of that novel's subject), while the content of the novel is something infinitely more complex.

THE SIGNIFICANCE OF SUBJECT: It should be clear from what has been said that no subject, as we are using the term, is good or bad in itself. The problems of middle-class women existed before Flaubert chose them for his subject and would have existed had he never chosen them. These problems in themselves could provide subjects for an indefinite number of novels, some excellent, some atrocious, some mediocre. Therefore, if *Madame Bovary* is, as most critics attest, a superior novel, then, that is not to be attributed to the superiority of its subject.

SUBJECT AND THE READER: Yet it is undeniable that some readers, while perhaps agreeing that you can't tell a book by its cover, do tend to select books by their subjects. One reader may like to read stories about young love but won't read anything on the subject of war, while another reader's tastes may be exactly the reverse. I once recommended a movie to a very intelligent friend of mine, and he replied that he didn't think he'd see it because he didn't like movies about doctors. I pointed out to my friend, an ardent admirer of Herman Melville's *Moby Dick*, that this was rather like saying one doesn't like novels about white whales, but he remained unconvinced.

This kind of prejudice, for that is what it is, is unfortunate. Readers who succumb to it are needlessly cutting themselves off from many of the pleasures that good literature (and good movies) can give. It is wisest to grant to the writer the authority to choose the subject; our project as readers is to see how subject is transformed into content. That is, judge the story, not the subject.

SUBJECT AND THE WRITER: But if no subject is good or bad in itself, a subject may be good or bad for a particular writer. We may assume that every writer will find there are some subjects he or she cannot transform into content, some subjects he or she is incapable of turning into stories. On the other hand, the writer often will find that some subjects are particularly suited to his or her talents and temperament. Indeed, some writers (D. H. Lawrence, for one) seem to find a particularly congenial subject early in their careers and return to it again and again as they mature. It may be observed that some writers, even some very good ones, may have only one real subject in the entire body of their work. For the writer, the best subject is the one that calls forth the deepest and most intense artistic response—and that may mean simply the most fully human response. That is all, as regards the writer's subject, that we may legitimately ask.

THE EXAMPLE OF AUSTEN: The English novelist Jane Austen (1775–1817) is an excellent example of a writer who was wise in choice of subject. She lived in one of the most eventful periods in British history, but her own life, on the surface at least, was rather uneventful. As a novelist, she drew not on the Napoleonic wars, about which she was probably not especially well informed and of which she undoubtedly had no firsthand information, but on the quiet provincial life with which she was entirely familiar. For the sort of reader for whom subjects have some sort of intrinsic value, Austen's choice may seem foolish. Yet in not choosing the big subject that could have little personal meaning for her but the apparently smaller subject to which her complex, ironic personality more fully responded, Jane Austen was making the only choice a genuine novelist could make. And the proof that her choice was wise lies in the greatness of her novels, such as *Emma*, *Persuasion*, and *Pride and Prejudice*. Today Jane Austen is universally recognized as one of the greatest of English novelists.

FROM SUBJECT TO STORY: To judge a work of fiction by its subject, then, is as ill-advised as to judge a book by its cover. The true critical question is how the author transforms subject into content, into a story.

THE READER'S EXPECTATIONS: At this point it might be advisable to remind ourselves of what we commonly expect of a work of fiction. In specific details, the nature of these expectations will differ from reader to reader. Yet we will surely find one element common to every reader's expectations before a work of fiction. That is the expectation that the work will tell a story.

WHAT IS NARRATIVE?: But what precisely do we mean when we say that the work of fiction tells a story? Again, there are no doubt many possible answers to this question, but for many readers in our time and in our cultural tradition the expectation of story carries within it the idea of what we may call the "linear plot" as norm. Therefore, the pages immediately following will be concerned with the linear plot as the most familiar form of narrative structure. Later in the chapter, we'll consider some of the principal alternatives to the linear plot.

A work of fiction, as we normally understand it, deals with events that occur in temporal sequence—that is, one after another. The notion is of a sort of "line" of events—hence, the term *linear*. The story of a man's life, for example, will include his birth, his growing up, his adulthood (including work and marriage), his growing old, and his death. Obviously, these events occur over a period of time. More commonly, a work of fiction will deal with a more limited series of events. A young man and woman meet, are attracted to each other, consider marriage, quarrel, separate, patch up their differences, and marry at the end of the story. Or they patch up their differences but decide that marriage between them just wouldn't work, and that ends the perhaps more contemporary version of the story. In either version, the element of temporal sequence remains clear.

Yet any experienced reader of fiction knows there is more to it than this. A story deals with events that occur in temporal sequence, to be sure, but a slavish adherence to temporal sequence is rare in fiction of any degree of maturity and sophistication. Consider, for example, F. Scott Fitzgerald's novel *The Great Gatsby*. In this classic of American fiction, we are told of Gatsby who as a boy planned to "study needed inventions" and of the mature Gatsby shot to death in his swimming pool. Applying to the text what we think we know about the world and the people in it, we suppose, appropriately, that Gatsby was a boy before he was a man and that his death was, in strictly temporal terms, the last event of his life. Yet the passage that focuses on Gatsby as a boy does not appear in the text until after Gatsby has "died." The novel departs, in this and in other instances, from strict temporal sequence.

We may say, in fact, that almost every story involves some sort of departure from strict temporal sequence. At the very least, we must be prepared for gaps in the sequence. Structurally, Ernest Hemingway's story "The Killers" is a relatively straightforward story. There is none of the kind of juggling with time we have noted in *The Great Gatsby*. Yet even Hemingway, while keeping the story moving forward in time, selects some moments for inclusion and rejects others. What is presented or enacted happens in temporal sequence, but not everything is presented. There are gaps.

PLOT

THE NATURE OF PLOT: What this seems to imply is that the simple setting down of events in temporal sequence is not the only, or even the main, concern of the writer of fiction. Other things are more important. It is in arranging the events of the story according to demands other than the purely temporal that the author creates plot.

In other words, the linear plot aims to reveal events to us, not only in their temporal sequence but also in their causal relationships. And although our general understanding is that causes must precede their effects in time, good fiction demonstrates that our understanding of causal relationships may be enhanced by a departure from temporal sequence in the presentation of events. Whether such a departure occurs or not, a good linear plot makes us aware of events not merely as happening one after another but as forming an intricate pattern of cause and effect. Nick's decision at the end of "The Killers" to leave the town in which the story is set is one event in a series. But it is also the effect of the events that have preceded it, the implication of those events, and the impact of events and implications on Nick. Gatsby's death and dismal funeral in Fitzgerald's novel must be seen as the final effects in a causal chain that can be traced all the way back to Gatsby's boyhood. And as Fitzgerald's novel indicates, the writer of fiction is willing to boldly manipulate temporal relationships for the sake of revealing with the greatest force the causal relationships that are his or her principal concern.

In fiction, plot means not simply the events recounted in the story but the author's arrangement of those events. And we are suggesting that the arrangement of events we call the linear plot is often motivated by the desire to render most forcefully the causal relationships among the events.

THE STRUCTURE OF PLOT: To recognize this much, however, is only a beginning. We must consider in more specific terms the form a linear plot is likely to take; for, underlying the evident diversity of fiction, we may discern certain recurring patterns.

We may seem to be belaboring the obvious if we note that one discernible pattern is the division of the story into beginning, middle, and end. But if we remind ourselves that a story arises from a series of choices, this apparently crude division may come to seem rather more significant. The writer chooses to begin the story at one point and end it at another. And as we have seen, the writer need not feel bound by temporal sequence in moving from beginning through middle to end. The pattern of beginning-middle-end is therefore a pattern of choices— that is, a meaningful pattern.

BEGINNING: We expect a story to begin at the beginning. In a story like "The Killers," the beginning may be what comes first in time, but The Great Gatsby illustrates that this is not always so. What we want to know is what, besides temporal sequence, determines the choice of a beginning.

Rather than losing ourselves in abstractions at this point, let's examine the beginning—specifically, the first paragraph—of a very famous story, Nathaniel Hawthorne's "Young Goodman Brown."

> Young Goodman Brown came forth at sunset into the street at Salem village; but put his head back, after crossing the threshold, to exchange a parting kiss with his young wife. And Faith, as the wife was aptly named, thrust her own pretty head into the street, letting the wind play with the pink ribbons of her cap while she called to Goodman Brown.

EXPOSITION: The first thing we may note about this paragraph is that it provides us with a certain amount of information. We are introduced to the story's title character; we are informed that he has a wife; we are told that like her husband she is young, and we are told that she is pretty. We are also informed that Brown and his wife live in Salem village. Drawing on our wordly knowledge, we recall that Salem is the name of a city in Massachusetts. The word "village," however, indicates the historical setting of the story. It takes place before Salem became a city. Finally, we are informed that Goodman Brown is parting from his wife. We are not told at this point whether he is going on a long and hazardous journey or a trivial errand. This information is given a bit later in the story; neither here nor in most stories is the beginning limited to a single paragraph.

Exposition is the name usually given to the process by which the writer imparts to the reader information necessary to the understanding of the story. Exposition is normally a primary function of the beginning of any story.

THE ELEMENT OF INSTABILITY: In fiction of any merit the beginning, however strictly expository it seems, implies more than the facts it presents. The situation with which the story begins, at least in the linear plot, must have a certain openness and must be capable of some sort of development or else there would be nowhere for the plot to go. In short, we may expect that the situation with which the story begins will contain within it a hidden or overt element of instability.

What evidence of instability, whether hidden or overt, do we find in the first paragraph of "Young Goodman Brown"? Apparently, Hawthorne is presenting a picture of an almost ideally happy marriage. We note, for instance, that the young husband even after starting out pauses to kiss his wife. Yet there are unsettling elements in this paragraph.

First of all, the young couple is parting. Again, we do not know at this point for how long they will be apart. Yet we know, as a matter of wordly knowledge, that any separation is a potential challenge to the stability of a relationship. Second, there is a certain amount of ambiguity in the presentation of the young wife. We are told she is aptly named Faith. Still, the image of the wind playing with the pink ribbons may strike us as disturbing. The detail of the pink ribbons, combined with the reference to her prettiness, may lead us to suspect that vanity is a trait of Faith's character, and vanity and faith (for remember, we have been told that her name is apt) seem an unstable mixture. Finally, the story is set in Salem village. A reasonably informed reader would be aware of the Salem witch hunts of the seventeenth century. Naturally, we wonder if witchcraft is to play a role in the story about to unfold.

In short, while the first paragraph of Hawthorne's story seems on a superficial first reading an almost idyllic picture of marital bliss, certain troubling details will make the competent reader aware of the potential instability of the situation. This awareness will, of course, become more precise as the story progresses. Eventually, the reader will see which of the potential sources of instability constitute the real threat to the apparent stability of the initial situation and what form this threat will take. As these points become clear, we move from the beginning to the middle of the story.

The beginning of a story, then, in addition to the necessary exposition in the narrow sense of the term—the imparting of information—gives us the picture of a situation in which there exist sources of instability that may at the outset be latent or overt. In these respects the beginning of "Young Goodman Brown" is typical. But it should not be concluded that the beginning of every story will be in all details like this one. Again, there are a number of choices available to the author.

CHOICE AND BEGINNINGS: The beginning of "Young Goodman Brown" is scenic, a term whose meaning will become clearer in a later chapter. For the moment let us merely observe that Hawthorne begins his story with the direct presentation of two characters in action, rather than with a more generalized sort of introductory passage. The beginning of "My Kinsman, Major Molineux," another story by Hawthorne, is quite different:

> After the kings of Great Britain had assumed the right of appointing the colonial governors, the measures of the latter seldom met with the ready and generous approbation, which had been paid to those of their predecessors, under the original charters. The people looked with most jealous scrutiny to the exercise of power, which did not emanate from themselves, and they usually rewarded the rulers with slender gratitude, for the compliances, by which, in softening their instructions from beyond the sea, they had incurred the reprehension of those who gave them. . . .

We see that the story is placed explicitly in an historical setting, which is presented to us in general terms before the introduction of any specific action or characters. Why Hawthorne chose one sort of beginning for "Young Goodman Brown" and another for "My Kinsman, Major Molineux" is not a question we need settle here. Both beginnings, we should note, fulfill an expository function while suggesting (more explicitly in "My Kinsman, Major Molineux") sources of instability in the initial situation.

THE MIDDLE—CONFLICT, COMPLICATION, CLIMAX: We move from the end of the beginning to the beginning of the middle as the elements tending toward instability in the initial situation group themselves into what we recognize as a pattern of conflict. In "Young Goodman Brown" this pattern emerges upon Brown's encounter with a strange man in the forest. Brown has been thinking of what is to happen that night and musing that knowledge of it would kill his wife Faith. The strange man has been expecting Brown and is, it seems, to be his companion for the evening. But Brown indicates that he wishes to return home. It is in Brown's attempt to resist the will of his companion that the conflict becomes evident.

Note that this conflict is related to the elements of instability we observed in the very first paragraph of the story. To be sure, the suggestion of weakness in Faith's character is not yet developed. But the possible dangers in a parting from loved ones are certainly involved in Goodman Brown's journey into a dark forest where terrible work is to be done. And the diabolical overtones of this must remind us of the hints of witchcraft we find in the Salem setting.

COMPLICATION AND CLIMAX: Just as a development toward conflict is latent in the initial situation, so is a development towards climax latent in the initial conflict. The movement from the initial statement of conflict to the climax is often referred to as complication. The climax is reached when the complication reaches its highest point of intensity, from which point the outcome of the story approaches inevitability.

In "Young Goodman Brown" the complication covers the movement of the half-resisting Brown to the diabolical rites in the heart of the forest to which the stranger (who is, it seems, the devil) has been leading him. It includes the process by which the hero's resistance is weakened, until he is on the verge of joining the converts to the diabolical religion whose rites are being celebrated. But the story's highest point of intensity, the actual climax, is still ahead. Brown discovers that Faith, the wife he had believed would be killed by the very thought of such evil practices, is herself among the communicants. And the story reaches its climax when, at the very moment they are about to be received into the communion, Brown cries to Faith to join him in resisting the evil one.

The importance of complication in the structure of the linear plot cannot be overestimated. Without adequate complication, the conflict would remain inert, its possibilities never realized. And it is by the control of complication that the writer gradually increases the intensity of the narrative, thus preparing us to receive the full impact of the climax. It is revealing that the greatest part of "Young Goodman Brown" is devoted to developing the complication. It seems that the invention and control of complication are of the highest importance in the creation of the linear plot.

THE END: In our three-part division of the linear plot, the end consists of everything from the climax to the *denouement* or outcome of the story. In "Young Goodman Brown" the end is devoted to the aftermath of Brown's experience in the forest. Shattered by what has happened, he lives out his life in misery, and, we are told, "his dying hour was gloom."

We began by discussing the structure of plot in terms of beginning, middle, and end. We may now see that the beginning takes us from exposition to the initial statement of conflict; the middle, from statement of conflict through complication to climax; and the end, from climax to denouement. And in a well-developed linear plot, the relationships among the three major parts, although they may at times be subtle, are nevertheless strongly defined. In the middle of Hawthorne's story, Brown's movement to the heart of the forest in spite of hesitations echoes his pausing at the threshold before finally taking his leave in the very first paragraph of the story. And we may recognize on reflection, that Faith's presence in the forest, though shocking to Brown and perhaps at first surprising to us, has been foreshadowed in such details as the pink ribbons on her cap, with their suggestion that she is not after all a perfect exemplar of Puritan austerity. And have not Brown's repeated reflections on the angelic nature of his wife given us some reason to suspect that he is in for some kind of shock? In short, the parts of the story combine to form a coherent whole.

A NOTE ON CONFLICT: We have been referring often to conflict. The conflicts with which fiction concerns itself are of many kinds. A story may deal with a conflict within a single character (e.g., desire vs. duty), a conflict between characters, a conflict between an individual and society, a conflict between human and nonhuman (e.g., nature or the supernatural), and so on. It may be sometimes illuminating to attempt to state the conflict of a story in terms appropriate to a sports event or court case, following an A versus B formula. Even where this proves difficult, the very difficulty may bring us to the heart of the story. On a first reading, the conflict in "Young Goodman Brown" may seem to be Brown versus the devil, but upon reflection we may decide that the real conflict is within Brown himself. That both possibilities occur to us may be very important to our understanding of the story as a whole.

THE LAWS OF PLOT

In forming the particular plot of the story, the writer may be expected to follow certain laws. When we speak of the laws observed in the construction of a linear plot, we do not, of course, mean laws of the sort passed by legislative bodies. We mean rather generalizations drawn from the practices of writers of fiction through the ages. To deviate from these laws is therefore not in any sense a crime. Still, we may expect that many writers of the future will continue to follow the basic principles observed by their great predecessors. And we should not be surprised to discover that apparent deviations from these laws will often turn out on closer inspection to be not deviations at all but new applications of the old principles.

PLAUSIBILITY: Of the laws governing plot in fiction one of the most important is certainly the law of plausibility. To say that a story seems to us plausible is simply to say that it is convincing on what we take to be its own terms.

There are, then, two steps involved in judging whether a story has plausibility. For before we can determine whether a story is convincing on its own terms, we must recognize what those terms are.

The demand for plausibility must not, for instance, be confused with the demand for realism. We are generally right in demanding that a story be plausible. But we have no right to demand that a story be realistic, for realism is only one of the many modes of fiction.

A story is plausible when it is true to itself. Skeptical readers may find it unrealistic that the devil appears as a character in "Young Goodman Brown." But even these readers must admit that if we accept the devil's direct intrusion in human affairs as a premise, the rest of the story is perfectly convincing.

Consider the denouement, for instance. Brown's "dying hour was gloom." Note how naturally this flows from what has gone before. Brown dies in gloom because he is unable to bear the insight into the sinful nature of humanity that he has gained in the forest. And this insight proves unbearable for Brown because before going into the forest he had an idealized, rather than realistic, view of human nature. This idealized view made him believe that Faith would be killed by the very thought of sin. And his extreme reaction to his new insight is entirely plausible; for just as Faith had seemed totally good before, now she seems totally evil. At the end of the story, as at the beginning, Brown is unable to accept the view, apparently implicit in his experience, that human nature is mixed. There is a deeper consistency underlying the superficial reversal in Brown's character and outlook. Thus, as is commonly the case in the linear plot, consistency of character is the basis of the story's plausibility, of its truth to itself.

SURPRISE: Plausibility, we have said, implies a story's truth to itself. This seems to suggest that a story's end is somehow contained in its beginning. In a sense this is true. At the same time a story that never surprises us is likely to prove rather dull reading. How then may the apparently contradictory claims of surprise and plausibility be reconciled?

An answer may be suggested by the simple example of the pure formal detective story. For example, at the end of the second-to-last chapter of a novel by Agatha Christie or Ngaio Marsh, when the murderer's identity is revealed, we want to be surprised. Indeed, if we are not surprised, we quite rightly consider this a flaw in the novel.

But then we turn to the last chapter. For a detective novel does not usually end with the identification of the murderer. After identifying the murderer, the great detective proceeds to explain by process of reasoning what has led to the solution. And now we want to be convinced that the solution that seemed so surprising was in fact inevitable and the only possible solution in the light of the evidence. And again, if this demand is not satisfied, we feel that the novel is flawed.

Now what is explicit, even at times mechanical, in the detective story is implicit in most good fiction. We want to be surprised, but then we want to be assured that the surprise does not violate the basic law of plausibility. Is it surprising that Faith is a participant in the dark rites of the forest? It is also plausible. After all, we are all sinners; certainly, we are none of us angels. And we are not asked to accept Faith's presence until it has been made clear that virtually the entire population of Salem, including the preacher and Brown's own parents, is also present. Finally, we recall that at the very beginning of the story we saw in the pink ribbons in Faith's cap the pathetic flag of her human frailty.

SUSPENSE: A third law governing plot is that a good plot arouses suspense. By suspense we mean an expectant uncertainty about further developments in the story, especially about the outcome or denouement. True suspense is more than a matter of not knowing how things will turn out. I don't know how things turn out in thousands of stories that I've never read, but I'm hardly in suspense about them. The suspense of which we speak involves some awareness of the possibilities and, ideally, some concern about them. Suspense develops as we become aware of the incipient instability in a situation. In "Young Goodman Brown," Brown heads into the forest; he may continue all the way to the heart of the forest, or he may turn back. The choices are not unlimited, and we have our expectations, but we are ultimately uncertain. With regard to Faith, we are in suspense as soon as we become aware that she may be in the forest. Our suspense as to this point is relieved when we learn for certain that she is there. But this knowledge, in turn, puts us further in suspense. We now have both Brown and Faith in the forest. What is to follow?

A device conducive to suspense is *foreshadowing*. By this we mean introducing details that hint at the direction the story is going to take. Hawthorne, for instance, introduces details that suggest Faith's presence before unambiguously revealing her presence to us. He thus builds up in us the expectation (not, however, the certainty) that she will be there; then he satisfies that expectation.

PLOT AND UNITY: The one overriding demand commonly made of the linear plot is that it have unity. It should be clear by now that a plot that fits the description we have been developing must inevitably have unity. A plot that has a true beginning, middle, and end that follows the laws of plausibility, surprise, and suspense must have unity.

It would be unfortunate if this analytic discussion of plot were taken to suggest that plotting is merely a mechanical process. In fact, plot is of the highest importance in lending a sense of meaning to fiction. Through plot the author organizes the raw material of experience. The ways authors organize experience tell us a great deal about their ways of understanding experience—that is, about the meanings experience has for them. Surely our sense of the meaning of experience is closely tied to our understanding of what causes what, and it is an important part of the work of plot to clarify causal relationships. To recognize the cause of Goodman Brown's dying gloom is to go a long way toward understanding his story.

ALTERNATIVE PLOTS

Although a good deal of what we have said so far is applicable to plot in general, our principal emphasis has been, as we indicated before, on the linear plot. In the remainder of this chapter we'll be considering some of the alternatives to the linear plot, as well as some of the ways in which the linear plot itself may allow for complexities that we haven't yet considered.

THE TELEOLOGICAL ASPECT: In our discussion of the plot of "Young Goodman Brown" our emphasis has been heavily on what some critics call the *teleological* aspect of plot. That is, we've tended to examine the various parts of the story very much in light of the end. Although we examined the beginning and middle—and, in fact, devoted more space to each of these than to the end itself—our orientation was always toward the end. Thus, our comments on the coherent whole that the parts of the plot combine to form, as well as our comments on unity, refer to aspects of plot that do not become entirely clear until we have arrived at the end of the story. The same is true of the concept of foreshadowing. We can, after all, recognize foreshadowing as such only in retrospect. Only when it is established that Faith is indeed in the forest do we recognize that her pink ribbons and her husband's insistence on her angelic nature have combined to foreshadow her presence there. The most that can occur before such confirmation is the active reader's more or less informed guess as to the direction the story is likely to take. Making such guesses is, of course, an important part of the reading process.

But the reading process is not entirely so end-oriented as these remarks may suggest. Of course, our curiosity as to how things will turn out and the steps by which we'll arrive at the outcome are important motives for continuing to turn the pages. But there's more to reading fiction than this, as even a short story like "Young Goodman Brown" will reveal.

THE EPISODIC ASPECT: When Young Goodman Brown and the devil conduct their debate in the forest—Brown expresses his reservations and hesitations and the devil slyly undermines Brown's position and thereby subtly weakens his resistance—the scene functions in part to bring Brown one step closer to the Satanic rites that are to be celebrated and to move the story one step closer to its outcome. Yet while serving this function in the story as a whole, the scene seems to take on a kind of life of its own. We feel a certain interest in the debate for its own sake. The cleverness of the devil's countermoves and the intriguingly sinister implications of his remarks (is there no one who remains outside the devil's party?) complicate our relation to the passage. On the one hand, there is the forward pull of our curiosity; on the other, our willingness to let the debate develop on its own terms at its own pace.

"Young Goodman Brown" remains a short story. One mark of the short story is that the end is not very far away from the beginning. In the short story there is relatively little leisure for the sort of development we've just been talking about. And indeed, the devil soon leaves Brown alone in the forest, bringing the debate to an end and permitting the story to go on its way. But we've received a glimpse of an interest that fiction may serve in addition to the teleological interest we emphasized before.

We'll call this second interest the *episodic* interest because it involves our interest in the episode for its intrinsic merits rather than for what it may contribute to the design of the whole and to the inexorable movement to the end. As we've already seen, the episodic interest may be engaged by what remains essentially a linear plot. In a short story constructed on the basis of the linear plot, though, this interest may be indulged only within relatively severe limits, as in "Young Goodman Brown." Longer narrative forms more easily permit fuller play to the episodic interest, as the episodes of the narrative may be developed in greater detail. When the narrative as a whole seems designed primarily to satisfy the episodic, rather than the teleological interest, then we may speak of the episodic as distinguished from the linear plot.

The episodic plot, in which interest in the episode takes precedence over interest in the progression of the whole to a resolution, is a major alternative to the linear plot. As what we have already seen should suggest, the distinction between linear and episodic plot is not always a hard and fast one. In the linear plot of "Young Goodman Brown" the episodic interest is present but undeveloped. Our interest in what we've called the debate is real, but it is not allowed to impede the forward, linear progression of the plot. In the same way, plots in which the episodic interest is developed to a very high degree don't always renounce entirely the teleological interest we associate more strongly with the linear plot.

Consider, for example, Mark Twain's *Adventures of Huckleberry Finn*. For most readers, this novel is what the title suggests it is—the account of a series of adventures, linked primarily by the fact that all of them involve the character Huckleberry Finn. As we move through such episodes as the Shepherdson-Grangerford feud, the attempt to lynch Colonel Sherburn, and the antics of the Duke and the Dauphin, it's not surprising if few of us give much thought to where all this is leading us. Certainly these episodes, all claiming our interest in themselves, hardly strike us as forming collectively the complication arising out of a conflict and leading to the climax and resolution. It is the teleological interest that seems weaker in this text.

The Adventures of Huckleberry Finn is for most of us an example of the episodic plot. And yet the teleological interest has not entirely disappeared. Early in the novel we meet the slave Jim, who soon joins forces with Huck after running away to avoid being sold down the river. The question of Jim's fate is not the center of our attention at all times as we read the novel, but it's never completely forgotten either. And the novel doesn't come to an end until we learn what that fate is. If *Huckleberry Finn* exemplifies the episodic plot, it's because in Mark Twain's novel the episodic interest has become dominant, not because the teleological interest plays no part.

In a more recent novel, David Bradley's *Chaneyville Incident*, the teleological interest of the linear plot seems clearly dominant. The protagonist is led, step-by-step, to the answers to questions that enable a resolution of the basic conflict defined early in the text—essentially, a conflict within the character himself. But along the way to these final answers, the character hears, tells, and tries to piece together stories of his father, his father's friends, the "old days," racism, slavery, and the Underground Railroad. Many of these stories, while they play a part in the gradual process of illumination in which the character is engaged, also hold considerable interest in themselves. In this case, the dominance of the teleological interest, while indicating that we are dealing with a primarily linear plot, doesn't entirely cancel out the episodic interest.

Novels like *The Great Gatsby* and Hawthorne's *Scarlet Letter* are even more strongly linear, reminding us that the strongly linear plot is not found only in the short story. And, of course, *Huckleberry Finn* by no means represents the outer limits of the episodic plot. *The Adventures of Don Quixote*, an important influence on Mark Twain, is more "open" and fully episodic than *Huckleberry Finn*, ending not with the resolution of a plot issue but only with the death of the hero.

Many classics of literary modernism, not often discussed in terms of plot by critics, might usefully be approached by way of the concept of the episodic interest. Leopold Bloom's wanderings around Dublin in James Joyce's *Ulysses* provide one promising example. The notorious lack of closure, the apparently deliberate refusal to bring issues to resolution, in Virginia Woolf's *Mrs. Dalloway* suggest that the primary appeal of this novel, at the level of plot, is in episodic interest.

The most obvious examples of the episodic plot seem to come from longer narratives, which is not surprising in view of the opportunities for fuller development afforded by longer forms. But the episodic plot may be found in the short story as well and seems to occur often in those contemporary stories sometimes classified as "postmodern." In Donald Barthelme's "Views of My Father Weeping," a young man sets out in search of facts about the violent death of his father. He is given several accounts of the "accident" that refuse to add up to a coherent whole. The story of his search is periodically interrupted by passages that provide anecdotes of a sort about the father, without relating clearly to the rest of the text or to our worldly knowledge of fathers and their ways. The young man is finally given a circumstantial account of the incident, only to be told that the source of this account is a "bloody liar." This brings us to the last word of the story, a word that obviously resolves nothing: "Etc."

Again, there is the rejection of closure, the refusal to bring issues to a resolution. This is in part what leads us to see the plot here as episodic rather than linear. But it could be argued that more is involved here.

It is not merely that the teleological interest is not finally satisfied. The episodic interest is more than a little frustrated as well. The episodes seem undetermined in themselves. What sense can we make of the father's drawing happy faces in the icing of cupcakes? Or for that matter, of father and son on a hunting trip, shooting peccadilloes? It's not, therefore, just a matter of the episodes not adding up. The episodes in themselves seem to refuse our efforts to assimilate them to our normal ways of making sense.

PLOTLESS FICTION: This suggests we are approaching a third term in our classification of plot types. We seem, in fact, to be moving toward what might be called *plotless fiction*. Notions such as causality, which we were dealing with so confidently just a few pages back, seem to have become problematic. In a story like "Views of My Father Weeping," what causes what? What indeed is the *subject* of the story, in the sense we used earlier—that is, to what does the story refer? Does the notion of reference apply here at all?

We aren't going to try to answer these questions here and now. We are simply going to address ourselves briefly to the troubling question of plotlessness in fiction. What does it mean to say that a story like "Views of My Father Weeping" may be plotless? Apparently, we're saying that the story deliberately (so we assume) undermines certain expectations that we bring to it. Yet this doesn't mean that those expectations are irrelevant to the story. Doesn't a story like this one work precisely by anticipating the reader's expectations and then systematically undermining them? And doesn't this suggest that such a story depends at least in part for its impact on the very expectations that it undermines? In short, isn't the plotless story a meaningful option for the writer only so long as plot remains a meaningful concept for the reader? Whether the plotless story can ever become the norm, I don't know. In fact, I confess I can't imagine what that would mean. For the present at least, it seems that even when the project at hand is the understanding of a plotless story, we still must bring to it some understanding of plot.

CHAPTER TWO
CHARACTER

INTRODUCTION: In the preceding chapter we saw that plot results from a series of choices made by the author. Another way of saying the same thing is that plot is artificial. In life we experience events and these events happen in some kind of sequence, but the patterning of events that is plot belongs to fiction. Plot is the imposition of form on experience that is in itself, at least as we normally perceive it, essentially formless.

Now, even the reader who has never before thought of the question in precisely these terms will probably have little difficulty in accepting this view of plot. We are all really aware, however vaguely, that plot is artificial, that it is something made up.

The reader may find it more difficult, however, to think of character in these terms. For if there are no plots in life, there are certainly people. And most of us expect the people—or *characters*—in fiction to be similar to the people in life. To call a fictional character "artificial" is usually to imply disapproval. Whatever degree of artifice we are willing to allow in plot, we expect characters to be "natural" or "lifelike."

LIFELIKENESS

THE STANDARD OF LIFELIKENESS: It is the argument of this chapter that the criterion of lifelikeness is inadequate for judging and understanding character in fiction. At best the notion of lifelikeness is an oversimplification. A fictional character must be other things besides lifelike, and the standard of lifelikeness doesn't help us to understand very much about the ways in which character is presented to us in fiction.

In reaction against what they see as an excessive emphasis on such qualities as lifelikeness, some critics have questioned whether there is any value in discussing fictional characters in terms of their alleged relationships to the human beings we encounter in the "real world." What these critics suggest is that we stop seeing fictional characters as people or representations of people and see them rather as functions. In this view, the only legitimate question we may ask of a fictional character, or of any trait or aspect of such a character, is what is it doing here, what does it contribute to the text of which it is a part?

The discussion that follows, while sympathetic to the view outlined in the paragraph above, tries to avoid its either/or reductionism. The view developed here is that a proper understanding of character in fiction requires a kind of dual awareness. We must simultaneously acknowledge the role of character as representation and as function. Beyond that general principle we must be guided by the text we're dealing with.

Even granting, then, that fictional characters are in part representations of people, we still assert that the standard of lifelikeness, in addition to being an oversimplification, may be downright misleading, especially if taken too literally. That is, the search for lifelikeness may lead the reader to overlook much that is essential in literary characterization.

Just what do we mean when we say that a character should be lifelike? What kind of life should a character be like? If we insist that characters should be like the people we know, aren't we imposing an excessively severe limitation on the author's creative powers? Would the great characters of fiction meet this test? Would Don Quixote? Ahab in *Moby Dick*? Cathy and Heathcliff in *Wuthering Heights*?

Again, I am not suggesting that we should entirely ignore the relation between fictional characters and real human beings. Rather, I am saying we should recognize that this relationship is a complex, not a simple one. In short, we must be aware not only of the similarities but also of the differences between fictional characters and real human beings.

CHARACTER AND FREEDOM: Whatever is true of the amount of freedom human beings enjoy, the fictional character is never entirely free; for, unlike the real human being, the fictional character is part of an artistic whole and must always serve the needs of that whole. One of the most delicate tasks of the writer of fiction is to create and maintain the illusion that the characters are free, while at the same time making sure that they are not really so. For a really free character would be free of his duties to the story of which he is a part, and a story that admitted such freedom could never achieve completeness and integrity as a story. Muriel Spark, in her novel *The Comforters*, has written amusingly of a group of characters who try to liberate themselves from the demands of plot and authorial intention. They fail. The necessity of being fitted into a satisfying whole is the most important difference between the fictional character and the human being and is the basis of all the other differences.

CHARACTER AND CHOICE: It is not enough, then, for the writer to have some capacity and opportunity for observing human beings in action and on the basis of those observations to imagine lifelike characters. The necessity of placing the character in a unified work of art—generally the writer's goal—forces the author into a series of choices. It may often be necessary to sacrifice one interest—for instance, the lifelikeness of character for its own sake—for the sake of others, such as plot, theme, and the unity of the whole. At the same time, the author must make sure that the choices do not become too obvious, do not impose themselves too assertively on the consciousness of the reader, for the focus of the reader's attention is supposed to be on the story, not on the difficulty the author had in writing it.

THE STANDARD OF RELEVANCE: Any discussion of character in fiction, therefore, must attend to the relationships between character and the other elements of the story and between character and the story as a whole. That is, character must be considered, analyzed, and discussed as part of the story's internal structure.

But just as we may ultimately refer the story as a whole to the real world in which we live our lives, relating the story to what we've called our worldly knowledge, so we may refer character to the real human beings who inhabit that world. Essentially, we refer fictional characters to ourselves: I am the human being I know best.

At this point the standard of lifelikeness may seem to suggest itself once again. But the limitations of that standard should now be even clearer than before. For if we ask that characters be like ourselves or like the people we know, we are not only setting boundaries on the writer's imagination, but we may also be overlooking the function of character within the story.

More to the point than the standard of lifelikeness is the standard of relevance. According to this standard, the question is not whether the character is like me. Rather, the question is, what has the character to do with me? In other words, what is the character's relevance to me?

UNIVERSAL AND PARTICULAR: The advantage of the standard of relevance is that it allows the author the full measure of freedom in the creation of character without denying the vital point of contact between the character and the reader. Theoretically, the author can range from the pure type, representing one universal quality, to the most eccentric of individuals. The author is bound only by the reader's demand that the character be in some way relevant to his or her experience.

It should be noted that a character may be far removed from the "normal" or the "average" without thereby becoming irrelevant to the reader. In William Faulkner's novel *The Sound and the Fury*, Benjy, one of the principal characters, is literally an idiot. An important part of the novel is told from Benjy's point of view. The standard of lifelikeness would be for most of us of little help in judging Faulkner's success in portraying Benjy. How can readers who are not themselves idiots determine whether Faulkner faithfully portrays the workings of an idiot's mind? If Faulkner's portrayal of Benjy is generally admired, it is because most readers recognize the relevance of Benjy.

FORMS OF RELEVANCE: What do we mean when we say that a character as different from the average reader as Benjy can still be relevant to that reader? There are essentially two ways in which a character can be relevant.

Characters are obviously relevant to us and to our experience if they are like ourselves or like others whom we know; lifelikeness is one form of relevance. A character is relevant if there are a lot of people like that in the real world.

But as we have already noted, the world does not contain many Don Quixotes, Ahabs, Cathy Earnshaws, or Heathcliffs. Are these characters, so often numbered among the great literary creations, irrelevant to us? If so, then either the standard of relevance is worthless or the critical judgment of generations has been mistaken.

What we must do is to recognize a second form of relevance. There are not many Don Quixotes or Cathy Earnshaws around, but there is something of Don Quixote and of Cathy Earnshaw in almost all of us. It is in this sense that we feel their relevance to us. And it may be that this form of relevance, rather than lifelikeness, is the secret of the power the great characters of fiction hold for us.

JUDGING FICTIONAL CHARACTERS: In judging fictional characters, there are certain questions that seem appropriate. Two of the most important are: What is the relevance of this character to me? In what ways does this character contribute to the story as a whole? Any judgment that ignores either of these questions will probably be inadequate.

SIMPLE AND COMPLEX CHARACTERS

The preceding paragraph suggests standards for judging fictional characters. But before these or any other standards may be responsibly applied, it is necessary to examine more closely the portrayal of character in fiction. We have to know more about the kinds of characters that appear in fiction and about the means by which character is portrayed.

With regard to the kinds of characters portrayed, it may be helpful to follow the practice of many critics and divide the characters of fiction into two general categories. That such a division is possible, even though it must always be applied carefully and with a full respect for the complexities of the text, serves to remind us of the artificiality of fictional characters. Few of us would claim that real human beings can be so categorized.

Our names for the two categories we are using will be simple characters and complex characters. Other critics, in making essentially the same division, sometimes use different terms. One of the most suggestive and influential statements of the distinction we have in mind is that of E. M. Forster, who in his *Aspects of the Novel* divides the characters of fiction into the "flat" and the "round."

SIMPLE (FLAT) CHARACTERS: The simple, or flat, character generally possesses just one dominant trait, or at most very few traits in clear and simple relationship to one another; he or she often seems less the representation of a human personality than the embodiment of a single attitude or obsession. Forster calls this kind of character flat because we see only one side of the character.

Included among simple characters are all the familiar types or stereotypes of fiction. The mark of the stereotyped character is the ease with which it can be reduced to a formula: the noble savage, the trusted old family retainer, and the poor but honest working girl are a few familiar fictional types.

Not all simple characters, however, are stereotypes like those referred to above. The essence of the stereotype may be expressed in a formula applicable to a large number of fictional characters, drawn from a large number of works of fiction. We must recognize the existence of a second kind of simple character. Like the stereotype, this kind of character may be summed up in a formula. But this character differs from the stereotype in that the formula is one of a kind; there is no other character in fiction with whom it exactly fits.

AN EXAMPLE FROM DICKENS: The works of Charles Dickens are filled with examples of this second kind of simple character. Consider, for instance, Uriah Heep in Dickens's novel *David Copperfield*. Uriah is certainly a simple character; his "personality" is made up of very few traits. In fact, he may be described as no more than an embodiment of his particular kind of "humility." The point is that his humility is of a particular kind. Uriah Heep is a simple character, but he is not a stereotype, because there is no one else quite like him in fiction.

COMPLEX (ROUND) CHARACTERS: At the other end of the spectrum is the complex character, called "round" by Forster because we see all sides of this character. The complex character, we may affirm, is more lifelike than the simple character because in life people are not simply embodiments of single attitudes. It is not surprising, therefore, that many of the most admired characters in fiction are complex characters. If Dickens is a master of the simple character, most of the great English novelists excel in portraying complex characters. Becky Sharp, the protagonist of Thackeray's *Vanity Fair*, is one example of a round character; her husband Rawdon Crawley is another. In fact, *Vanity Fair* abounds in brilliantly portrayed complex characters.

The simple character, we have said, may often be summed up in a formula; the complex character, by contrast, is capable of surprising us. Rawdon Crawley's deepening sense of responsibility in *Vanity Fair*, for instance, surprises us in the light of the first impression he makes. But surprise in character as in plot does not depend on the violation of plausibility if it is to be fully convincing. Thackeray's portrayal of Rawdon Crawley is one of the great examples in English fiction of a novelist convincing us of profound changes in one of his characters. And his success is based in large part on our awareness (which may become fully conscious awareness only in the process of analysis) that the seeds of change, and of precisely this kind of change, have been present in Rawdon from the start.

GRADATIONS IN COMPLEXITY: In contrasting simple and complex characters I used the metaphor of the spectrum. This was not acciden-tal. For characters in fiction should not be thought of as existing in sealed compartments, one marked "simple," the other "complex." The metaphor of the spectrum, connoting subtle gradations as we move from the simple to the complex, is more to the point. Captain Ahab in Melville's *Moby Dick* is certainly closer to the simple than to the complex end of the spectrum, but he is not, like many of the stereo-types of boys' fiction, an absolutely simple character. Although he unswervingly pursues a single goal throughout the novel and is in this respect a simple character, he is capable of at least some hesitation, self-doubt, or internal division and therefore tends toward complexity. He doesn't surprise us; he never abandons his search for the whale. But his self-awareness, his full and defiant consciousness of the obsessive nature of his behavior, lends him some degree of complexity. In the same novel, Ishmael and Starbuck are more complex than Ahab, yet neither is equal in complexity to Becky Sharp and Rawdon Crawley. Complexity is a matter of degree; a character may be more or less complex.

FUNCTION OF COMPLEX CHARACTERS: Should a writer aim for complexity or simplicity in the portrayal of character? It is often suggested (by Forster, among others) that the complex or round character is a higher kind of achievement than the simple. This view must be seriously qualified as we shall see. But let's begin by examining the functions that can best be served by the complex character.

COMPLEXITY AND RELEVANCE: Complex characters are more lifelike than simple characters and, as we have seen, lifelikeness is to be valued as one form of relevance. No real human being can be summed up in a formula, as a simple character can. Certainly I, the reader of fiction, would be most unwilling to admit that I can be so summed up. Real human beings are capable of surprising us. The complex character can surprise us; the simple character cannot. Therefore, we may conclude that complexity of character tends to produce lifelikeness in fiction.

COMPLEXITY AND CRAFTSMANSHIP: There is another basis for the admiration critics often express for the well-drawn complex character. As an achievement in literary craftsmanship, the complex character is in many ways more difficult than the simple one. The simple character need only repeat the formula at each appearance. Revealing a character's complexity to the reader, on the other hand, is an immensely complicated business. The writer and the reader must remember that complexity is not to be achieved at the price of coherence. It is not enough that the complex character not have a formula and that the character acts differently at different points in the story. The complexity we want is in most cases the complexity of the unified character. The writer must satisfy simultaneously our demand for complexity and our demand for unity. This is why writers are sometimes attacked for letting the personages they have created behave "out of character," that is, in a manner inconsistent with what has already been established about them. To behave in this way lends a character some kind of complexity, perhaps, but at the cost of unity. If we did not feel that the Rawdon Crawley we come to know in the early scenes of *Vanity Fair* was capable of becoming the Rawdon Crawley of the later scenes, he would be in this respect a failure as a character. It is the combination of complexity and unity, the sense of unity in complexity that is impressive.

CONSISTENCY: It may be objected at this point that since human beings often act inconsistently (it's one of the ways they surprise us), there is no reason to demand unity of fictional characters. There are several possible answers to this objection. First, it is not certain that human beings do act inconsistently. The apparent inconsistencies of human behavior may simply indicate the limits of our knowledge of ourselves and of others. Seen in the right perspective—in the eye of God or the psychoanalyst, for example—we may all behave more consistently than we know.

But we need not retreat to metaphysics or to psychoanalysis to settle this problem. We need only remind ourselves that the fictional character, however complex, is not a human being; the fictional character is an artistic creation, part of an artistic whole. And we traditionally demand of art a sense of form that we neither find nor expect to find in life. This sense of form is, in fact, quite possibly the essential difference between art and the rest of life. Briefly, when we praise a fictional character for being lifelike, we must remember that this is not an adjective we would apply to an actual living person. A thing cannot be lifelike unless it is really not alive.

Finally, it may be pointed out that the writer of fiction can depict inconsistency in human behavior. But as Aristotle advises in his *Poetics*, let the inconsistent character be consistently inconsistent. Inconsistency should not be something the writer resorts to simply as a way of getting out of plot difficulties, as when the wicked uncle has a change of heart in the last chapter so that the story may come to an otherwise impossible, and still incredible, happy ending.

FUNCTIONS OF SIMPLE CHARACTERS: Consistency and unity should present no problem where the simple character is concerned, for the simple character is by definition consistent. What many readers object to in simple characters is that they are consistent at the price of complexity and their lack of complexity violates our sense of the human personality. There is some truth to this charge, but we must recognize that the simple character can perform important functions in the work of fiction.

SIMPLICITY AND LIFELIKENESS: We have said that, because human beings are complex, complex characters are more lifelike than simple characters. Now we must see that simple characters can make an important contribution to the overall lifelikeness of a work of fiction.

The fact is, if I think of my life as a story, I find it contains more simple than complex characters. Does this contradict what we've been saying about the complexity of the human personality? Not really. Again, it's a matter of perspective.

In the story of my life, I am the most complex character. This doesn't mean, of course, that I am really more complex than other people but that I am more aware of my own complexities than of the complexities of other people. I know myself from the inside, others only from the outside.

Still, among the others there are some I know quite well. These include, I suppose, my immediate family and my closest friends. I can't know them as well as I know myself, but I can be aware of some of their complexities.

And then there are the other "others," ranging from casual acquaintances to people I pass in the street. In the eye of God, no doubt, each of these is a highly complex personality, but in my eyes they are simple characters. Whatever they may have in the way of complexity I know little or nothing about.

And this brings us to the connection between between the simple character and lifelikeness. The use of simple characters to fulfill minor roles in a work of fiction satisfies my sense of life, not perhaps as it really is (the eye of God again), but as I experience it. The simple character can serve very well as a minor character in fiction, contributing to our sense of the overall lifelikeness of the story.

SIMPLICITY AND IMAGINATION: But the simple character is not limited in fiction to use as a minor character, part of the background against which the main action is played out. Captain Ahab, protagonist of Melville's *Moby Dick*, is essentially a simple character, as are many of the principal characters in Dickens. Is a writer justified in casting the simple character in the role of protagonist or principal character?

We must first of all distinguish between the stereotyped simple character (the poor but honest working girl) and the individualized simple character (Ahab, Uriah Heep). Stereotypes are substitutes for imagination; the individualized simple character is an original imaginative creation. Except in very special circumstances—say, when character is only a minor interest in a work whose main emphasis is elsewhere—stereotypes will appear as major characters only in fiction of a very low order of sophistication. But the individualized simple character may be an imaginative accomplishment worthy to take a central position in fiction of the very highest order.

Again, we must remind ourselves that relevance, rather than lifelikeness, is the important standard. Ahab is not lifelike. I have never met anyone like him, and I trust I never shall. But in Ahab's total commitment to an obsession I recognize a part of myself. That is the secret of his relevance, of his power. That is why, in spite of his relative simplicity, he can stand at the very center of a major work of fiction.

We may now make a few tentative generalizations. Insofar as the author's end is realism, in the sense of the accurate representation of the surface of life, we may expect that the principal characters will be complex. The simple character is more likely to appear in a major role as the writer moves away from realism in the direction of expressionism and fantasy. Thackeray, the realist, gives us complex characters, while Melville, the symbolic romancer, gives us a simple character as protagonist. Finally, that kind of simple character we call the stereotype may appear in a minor role in serious fiction but will, as a general rule, play a major role only in inferior fiction.

EVALUATION OF CHARACTER TYPES: It is an oversimplification to assert without qualification that the complex character is a greater achievement than the simple character. If we think of character in itself, divorced from all of the other elements of fiction, we may place a high value on complexity. But if we examine character in the light of the story as a whole, we must see that complexity is not necessarily a greater virtue than simplicity. We must always ask what the character contributes to the story and what is the character's function.

CHARACTER TRAITS

Central to the kind of consideration of character in which we are now engaged is the notion of the *trait*. We've been using the term in accordance with Seymour Chatman's definition in his book *Story and Discourse*. A trait is a "relatively stable or abiding personal quality." Insofar as a trait is "stable or abiding," it is not so transient as, say, a mood. But its stability is relative. That is, a trait may undergo changes in degree, as when a character becomes less optimistic with the passage of time. And in more extreme cases one of a character's traits may disappear, or a character may in the course of the story develop new traits. The traits that combine to make up the whole character may conveniently be thought of as coming under three headings, to which we'll give the names *social, physical,* and *psychological.*

SOCIAL TRAITS: A character's social traits are those that have to do with the character's place in society, especially the character's relationship to groups and institutions constituted or recognized, or both, by society. To what social class, for instance, does the character belong? What are the character's political and religious affiliations? What, if anything, does the character do for a living? What is the character's marital status? What sort of family ties does the character maintain? Questions like these help to define the character's social traits.

PHYSICAL TRAITS: When we ask whether the character is tall or short, young or old, fat or thin, blue-eyed or brown-eyed, it's obviously another kind of trait with which we are concerned. These questions and others like them lead us to an identification of the character's physical traits.

PSYCHOLOGICAL TRAITS: All of those traits, all of those relatively stable or abiding personal qualities that are neither social nor physical are, for us, psychological. Primarily, a character's psychological traits are the "inner" traits. Is the character emotional or intellectual, optimistic or pessimistic, secure or insecure? In some cases, characters may seem to illustrate theories of human psychology like those associated with Sigmund Freud. And in our sense of the term, psychological traits may include, in addition to the "inner" traits, characteristic patterns of external observable behavior, such as rhythms of speech, qualities of gesture, and so on. To qualify as a trait, a gesture must be part of a characteristic pattern, not simply an isolated instance. Thus, if my nose is itchy and I scratch it to make the itch go away, that's an isolated instance rather than a trait of my character. But if I scratch my nose with significant frequency, either under any and all circumstances or under certain predictable circumstances—say, in highly formal surroundings—it may be appropriate to regard nose-scratching as one of the traits of my character. If, on the other hand, I would never scratch my nose, no matter what the circumstances or how severe the itch, that may also be a psychological trait. Or at any rate, it may point to a trait.

RELATIONSHIPS AMONG TRAITS: We may, then, approach the characters of fiction in terms of these three kinds of traits. But simply checking off traits is not the same as understanding a character. It is through the combination of traits that character is formed, and that means that in dealing with a fictional character we must deal not only with these three classes of traits in isolation from one another but also with the relationships among the three classes. We must be prepared to ask such questions as to what extent a character's psychological traits may be the product of the character's social traits. "The very rich," F. Scott Fitzgerald said, "are different from you and me," suggesting that for at least one American author the psychological cannot be separated from the social.

Fitzgerald's comment further suggests that for him social traits are important in defining character. One of the questions the reader may ask of any work of fiction is whether the author seems to give an unexpected or unusual weight to any one of the three classes of traits we've indicated over the others. Does the author so emphasize social traits as to suggest the view that people are to be understood as social rather than as physical or psychological beings? Or does the author tend to treat one class of traits as cause and another as effect, as when a character's political persuasion (social) seems the result of his deeply ingrained resentment of his father (psychological)?

Finally, we must recognize that the very act of deciding what kind of trait we're dealing with may prove more difficult than we suppose. If I note that a character is black, am I observing a physical trait or a social one? Certainly writers like Charles W. Chesnutt, David Bradley, and Toni Morrison have powerfully addressed the notion that being black is not simply a matter of pigmentation of the skin. And writers like Alice Walker, Marge Piercy, and Doris Lessing have reminded us forcefully that being a woman is not just a question of biology.

Traits, kinds of traits, and the relationships among them are thus vital in our understanding of character. And what we've been saying should make quite clear that examining characters in terms of their traits cannot be adequately done mechanically and is no simple matter. But the very difficulty we may experience in such an effort contributes to a deeper understanding of the fictional character and may, I venture to suggest, contribute as well to a greater understanding of what it is to be human—the kind of understanding, some would argue, that fiction exists to give us.

METHODS OF CHARACTERIZATION

The author's choices with regard to character do not end with the assignment of traits. The author must also choose methods of characterization, the methods by which the characters will be presented to the reader. There are a number of methods available to the author, each with its advantages. We shall classify these as the discursive, the dramatic, and the contextual.

DISCURSIVE METHOD: The author who chooses the discursive method simply tells us about the characters. The author enumerates their traits and may even express approval or disapproval of them. The most obvious advantages of this method are directness and economy. It is the quickest and least ambiguous way of introducing character.

No one uses the discursive method better than Jane Austen. Here is a passage from her novel *Pride and Prejudice*:

> Mr. Bennet was so odd a mixture of quick parts, sarcastic humour, reserve, and caprice, that the experience of three-and-twenty years had been insufficient to make his wife under-

stand his character. *Her* mind was less difficult to develop. She was a woman of mean understanding, little information, and uncertain temper. When she was discontented, she fancied herself nervous. The business of her life was to get her daughters married; its solace was visiting and news.

The main business of this passage is to tell us some of the principal traits of Mrs. Bennet's character, while allowing something of Mr. Bennet's character to come through as well. And it is a mark of Austen's economy that after this short paragraph we feel that we have a pretty clear notion of the relationship of husband and wife.

While admiring the craft that Austen displays here, most modern writers and critics tend to resist the discursive method. It is, they believe, relatively mechanical and discourages the active participation of the reader. In responding to the discursive method, I as reader am not encouraged to react directly to the characters, to make up my own mind about them, as I must react to and make up my own mind about the real people I meet.

In fact, for many of our contemporaries the discursive method of characterization is intrinsically inferior to other methods. According to this view, the author should not *tell* us but *show* us. Like most critical generalizations, this one oversimplifies. The discursive method can be the best choice under certain circumstances, for certain purposes. By using the discursive method in the passage quoted, for example, Austen "places" precisely a character who might become tedious if developed in other terms. It seems to be part of Austen's point that Mrs. Bennet is the sort of person who can be summed up in this way—that is, not a very interesting person at all. And certainly the passage illustrates the economy and directness the author can achieve through the discursive method.

THE DRAMATIC METHOD: Economy and directness are always virtues, but they are not always the virtues appropriate to the situation. Therefore, the discursive method will not always serve. The principal alternative to the discursive method is the dramatic method, precisely the method of showing rather than telling.

In the dramatic method, the author allows the characters to reveal themselves to us through their words and actions. This, of course, is how character is revealed to us in drama; that is why we call this method dramatic. But it is also how people reveal themselves to us in life. In life there is no author around to tell us that Mr. X is generous. Rather, by observing what Mr. X does and says, we may conclude that

Mr. X is generous. It is the same with the fictional character presented dramatically.

The advantages of the dramatic method should be obvious. Compared to the discursive method, the dramatic is more lifelike and invites the reader's active participation in the story. The dramatic method has generally been preferred to the discursive by writers of fiction in the twentieth century.

This method, though, has its disadvantages. It is less economical than the discursive because to show takes longer than to tell. In a story in which the events of the plot rather than the characters are of primary importance, the dramatic method of characterization might well be excessively cumbersome. And although this method encourages the reader's active participation, it also increases the possibility of the reader's misjudging the character. This difficulty should, of course, not arise for the attentive reader, provided the author has sufficient skill in showing, and there are circumstances in which an author may deliberately provoke uncertainty and ambiguity in the reader's interpretation of character.

CHARACTERS ON OTHER CHARACTER: Included under the general heading of the dramatic method is the device of having one character in the story talk about another. The reader must remember, of course, that information received in this way is not necessarily reliable. What A says of B may tell us more about A than about B. The real question is who is being characterized—A, or B, or both at once?

In presenting character the author may tell; that's the discursive method. Or the author may show; that's the dramatic method. And the author may suggest; that's the contextual method.

THE CONTEXTUAL METHOD: By the contextual method we mean the device of suggesting character by the verbal context that surrounds a character. If a character is constantly described in terms appropriate to a beast of prey, I as the reader may well surmise that the author is trying to tell me something.

CHARACTERIZATION BY TRANSFERENCE: One variation on the contextual method is what might be called characterization by transference. It has sometimes been the practice of authors to suggest psychological traits of character by the presence of physical traits. Thus, in some novels of the nineteenth century, women with blond hair are commonly pure and innocent, while women with dark hair are more often passionate and interesting. See Rowena and Rebecca in Scott's *Ivanhoe* by way of illustration. On the other hand, in American hard-boiled fiction of the twentieth century, women with blond hair are often mendacious and murderous; see the works of Raymond Chandler. Obviously, it would be dangerous to be guided by such considerations in the real world, but a recognition of such conventions is sometimes essential to understanding what's going on in a work of fiction.

MOTIVATION: We have insisted throughout this discussion that character must always be seen as one element in a larger artistic whole. The point at which plot and character come together is what we mean by the term *motivation*. Plot to a great extent consists of what the characters do. Motivation is why they do it.

We may think of motivation as general or particular. General motivation covers such basic human drives as love, hunger, and greed. Particular motivation involves the individual applications of these basic drives. If the hero acts to impress the heroine, that is particular motivation and an application of such general motives as love and perhaps vanity. It is a mark of coherence in character and plot that the reader be able to identify both the general and particular motivation for the actions of the characters. It is part of the story's general plausibility that the motivation be adequate to the action. If a character kills, we should be satisfied that we know why he killed, and we should be satisfied that the "why" is an adequate reason, or at least that it would seem adequate to the character.

CONCLUSION: It should by now be clear that neither plot nor character is intrinsically dominant in fiction. Some texts emphasize one; some, the other. Perhaps we may conclude this chapter by recalling the question set forth by Henry James: "What is plot but the illustration of character; what is character but the determinant of plot?"

CHAPTER THREE
SETTING

INTRODUCTION: Everything that happens, happens somewhere at some time. The element of fiction that reveals the where and when of events is called setting. The setting of George Eliot's *Middlemarch* is an English town in the nineteenth century; that of Ernest Hemingway's *The Sun Also Rises* includes Paris, Pamplona, and several other spots in France and Spain in the 1920s. In other words, the term *setting* refers to the point in time and space at which the events of the plot occur.

If we think of fiction as essentially concerned with what people do and with what happens to them—that is, with character and plot—setting may seem of lesser interest and importance. To many of us, perhaps, the setting of a story is simply a background before which the really important things happen.

Yet we may realize upon reflection that the role of setting is not nearly so limited, and that this is true in life as well as in fiction. Setting often defines the significance of events and actions. What is inappropriate, even rebellious behavior in one setting may be appropriate, even conformist behavior in another. A student who appeared naked in a classroom would, we suppose, intend this as a provocative act; the same costume would take on an entirely different significance at a gathering of nudists. Language that might offend my elders may establish me as one of the gang at the local hangout. The informality of today's manners would, a few generations back, have been perceived as rudeness. One of our greatest critics, Kenneth Burke, has coined the phrase "scene-act ratio" to suggest that, at least where human beings are concerned, there is always a significant interrelationship of setting and action.

Reading with attention to setting is important if we're trying to understand what's going on in fiction. What the scene-act ratio is and how important it is are always legitimate questions to ask about a story. But there's more to it than this. In the previous chapter, we suggested that examining characters in fiction is a way of coming to a deeper and broader understanding of ourselves as human beings; that's why the question of the character's relevance to me is so important. But to be human is to be in time and place, to be situated. I am a twentieth-century American, and that shapes me, I am sure, in more ways than I'll ever consciously realize. I am confident, though, that responding to setting as an element of fiction sharpens my awareness of what it is to live in one time and place rather than another; it helps me to get a sense of who I am. And, by the way, this suggests the particular value I can derive from reading fiction set in times and places other than my own. Such fiction provides me with a perspective from which I may more clearly perceive my own situation.

NEUTRAL SETTINGS: In spite of the great importance we have just been attributing to setting as an element of fiction, it remains undeniably true that in some works of fiction, setting is little more than a reflection of the truth that things have to happen somewhere. The author, principally concerned with plot or character, sketches in only enough by way of setting to lend the requisite verisimilitude to the action. Much of the fiction in the popular magazines of a few decades ago, for instance, offered merely a vaguely contemporary setting, either urban or rural. Beyond providing this much information, the authors had no real interest in setting and did not encourage such an interest on the reader's part. In such a case, we may speak of the setting as "neutral."

The use of the neutral setting is by no means limited to slick commercial fiction. Henry Fielding's *Tom Jones*, certainly one of the great novels in English, reveals little positive interest in setting. An inn is an inn, Fielding seems to believe, and a barnyard is a barnyard. There is no reason to single out whatever qualities may make the inns and barnyards in one part of England different from their counterparts in other sections of the country.

LIMITS TO NEUTRALITY: Even in the work of a writer like Fielding, however, the neutrality of setting is not absolute. If his inns are typical inns and his barnyards typical barnyards, he still recognizes that some scenes are properly set in inns and others in barnyards. He recognizes the value of a certain appropriateness of setting to event.

The same is true in the kind of commercial fiction we were talking about before. If a story in a slick magazine has a rural setting, this sets up in the reader certain expectations regarding character and plot. To be sure, these expectations are often based on stereotypes of the crudest sort. Nevertheless, they indicate that an absolutely neutral setting is rare.

THE SPIRITUAL SETTING: The expectations aroused in us by a rural setting suggest that few settings are absolutely neutral because few settings are merely physical. For the modern American reader, a rural setting suggests not just grass, cows, and barns but certain values that we might as well call spiritual. As long as the setting is only vaguely and conventionally rural, the values suggested are likely to be vague and conventional as well. But as the physical setting becomes more specific and more vividly rendered, so does the spiritual setting.

By spiritual setting, we mean the values embodied in or implied by the physical setting. The phrase "a small midwestern town" may immediately suggest one set of values, while New York City suggests quite another. That this is true not only in fiction but extends beyond fiction may be seen from a court case of not too many years back. A judge awarded custody of a child to the child's grandparents on the grounds that the grandparents were "good, midwestern people." Apparently, "midwestern" had for the judge a spiritual as well as geographical significance.

REFINING THE SPIRITUAL SETTING: We would hardly expect a writer of any merit to accept the judge's easy identification of the midwestern with the virtuous. This is precisely the kind of stereotype the serious writer will try to avoid. The writer will also, of course, seek to avoid the kind of reverse stereotype that would make "midwestern" a term of abuse.

The serious writer will recognize, and will force us to recognize, that there is no easy relationship between a particular setting and virtue or vice. The good writer will often, by precise observation and careful rendering, refine the setting until we are made aware of the complex of conflicting values that may inhere in a particular place and time. George Eliot's portrayal of life in a Victorian English town in her novel *Middlemarch* is one of the highest achievements of this sort in English fiction.

SETTING AS DYNAMIC: What has been said should indicate that setting need not mean merely a static backdrop before which the action unfolds itself. Setting may thrust itself dynamically into the action, affecting events and being in turn affected by them, until setting seems to assume the role of a major character.

THE ELEMENTS OF SETTING: Looking over what has so far been said, we begin to get a sense of the elements of which setting is composed. They may be listed under four headings: (1) the actual geographical location, including topography, scenery, even the details of a room's interior; (2) the modes of day-to-day existence of the characters as a group; (3) the time in which the action takes place, for example, historical period, season of the year, even time of day; (4) the religious, moral, intellectual, social, and emotional environment.

FUNCTIONS OF SETTING

SETTING AS METAPHOR: We have thus far been limiting our discussion to the literal presentation of setting. Even what we have called spiritual setting does not essentially involve a departure from the literal, since it extends only to the observable, if intangible, effects that time and place may have on character and events. Now we shall discuss a use of setting that involves extraliteral elements.

Sometimes in fiction we encounter details of setting that seem to function as a projection or objectification of the characters or of a pervasive spiritual condition. For instance, the fog that lingers so oppressively in Charles Dickens's *Bleak House* serves as a kind of metaphor for the spiritual malaise and confusion of the characters. This is not the same as what we have called the spiritual setting. It is not the fog that has contributed to the characters' malaise. If anything, it is the other way around.

But not quite, of course. Only in fantasy could a writer ask us to believe that a character's internal state could create an external fog. The fog in *Bleak House* truly exists as the town does in *Middlemarch*. But George Eliot asks us to observe the spiritual and emotional effects of the town on the individual, while Dickens asks us to see the fog as a metaphor (i.e., an implied comparison) for the individual's spiritual and emotional state.

ATMOSPHERE: A further function of setting, related to but not identical with its metaphorical function, is the creation of atmosphere. Atmosphere has been more talked about than defined, and because it refers to the suggested rather than the stated, it may be impossible to define satisfactorily. One critic has described it suggestively as the air we breathe as we enter the world of the literary work. It is a kind of mood or emotional aura, suggested primarily by setting, that helps to establish and direct the reader's expectations. A suggestion of mystery and foreboding may be established, for instance, by a description of shapes dimly seen in the darkness. A stormy night carries with it one emotional aura; a sunny morning, another.

The close relationship that often exists between the function of setting in creating atmosphere and the function of setting as atmosphere may be seen if we refer again to the fog of *Bleak House*. We have seen that the fog serves as a metaphor for the spiritual and emotional state of the principal characters. But it also affects the reader; it is part of the air the reader breathes upon entering the world of Dickens's novel. And as such it contributes to the creation of atmosphere.

We should note the possibility of contrast and development in atmosphere. A cheerful atmosphere created by a bright, sunlit setting may serve as a contrast to the dark and troubled inner state of the character. Or the atmosphere may develop, perhaps deepening in the course of the story. Our increasing sense of foreboding as the hero walks into the darkening forest in Hawthorne's "Young Goodman Brown" is an example of a gradual and subtle shift in atmosphere.

SETTING AS THE DOMINANT ELEMENT: Like character, setting may be the element of primary importance in a particular story or even throughout the work of a particular author. Certainly in George Eliot's *Middlemarch*, the setting, particularly the spiritual setting, strikes us as at least as important as plot and character. In this novel and others like it, plot and character seem to exist primarily as a means of revealing the effects of setting on human life.

TIME AS THE DOMINANT ELEMENT: In many works of fiction, the time in which the action occurs is of the highest importance. This is especially true of historical fiction, like William Makepeace Thackeray's *Henry Esmond* or Charles Dickens's *Tale of Two Cities*. In the latter novel, the French Revolution and the terror that followed it affect the lives of all the characters.

The customs and moral conventions of a particular time, part of the spiritual setting, may be of great importance even in works of fiction that are not intentionally historical. Thomas Hardy gave his *Jude the Obscure* a contemporary setting; that is, he set it in his own period. Still, it is Jude's inability to find personal fulfillment within the moral framework or the spiritual setting of that particular period that is the basis of his tragedy. Because of the difference in perspective, we modern readers may in some respects be even more aware than Hardy of the role that time plays in his novel.

That the particular terms of a moral conflict, like the one we find in *Jude the Obscure*, are related to a particular period—for example, attitudes toward marriage, social class, and opportunity that have undergone some changes in the years since the novel was first published in 1896—does not necessarily mean that the work dramatizing this conflict lacks what we sometimes call universality; nor does it mean that the work has no relevance to the reader of our time. The pattern of frustrated rebellion depicted in *Jude the Obscure* remains relevant, even if it may take rather different forms in our time than in Hardy's. And if our time gives us a fresh perspective on *Jude the Obscure*, it may also be said that *Jude the Obscure* gives us a fresh perspective on our time.

It is sometimes the case that a work of fiction takes on added interest, or at any rate interest of a new kind as we move further away from the time of its original publication. Today we read novels like Fitzgerald's *The Great Gatsby* and Hemingway's *The Sun Also Rises* in part for their evocative images of a colorful era of the past—the 1920s. We obviously find in these texts qualities that were not there in the same way for the original readers of the novels, for whom the 1920s were the present.

PLACE AS THE DOMINANT ELEMENT: Works of fiction in which the spatial setting or place dominates are often classified as examples of local color or regionalism. The regionalist seeks to investigate the effects on character and event of a particular geographical setting— which means, of course, a spiritual as well as physical setting.

The regionalist's interest in what it is like to live in a particular place—say, the American South—does not mean that the work of the regionalist is irrelevant to any reader who doesn't happen to live in that place. As we've already suggested, the process of being influenced by the time and place in which one lives is a universal process. Moreover, we may well discern within the mores of a particular place further patterns of behavior that have some claim to being considered universal.

A number of writers have devoted all, or at least a substantial part, of their work in fiction to the depiction of life in a particular region. The United States has produced an especially impressive body of regionalist fiction. Willa Cather deals extensively and intensively with life on the Nebraska prairie in novels like My Antonia. The Grandissimes by George Washington Cable is an important novel of Southern life in the nineteenth century. Sarah Orne Jewett and Mary Wilkins Freeman are among the most significant writers of fiction devoted to life in New England.

The nineteenth-century English writer Anthony Trollope and the twentieth-century American William Faulkner are regionalists of a special kind. Each has created an imaginary region as a setting for his fiction. Barsetshire, the setting of such novels by Trollope as The Warden and Barsetshire Towers, and Yoknapatawpha County, setting of The Sound and the Fury and of many other works by Faulkner, will not be found on any map. Barsetshire is a composite of many British counties, while Yoknapatawpha is based on the actual county in Mississippi where Faulkner lived much of his life. Trollope, Faulkner, and Thomas Hardy in his novels set in Wessex liberate themselves from the literal while remaining true to the regionalist's concern for the effect of setting on character and incident.

SETTING IN NONREALISTIC FICTION: When we speak of liberation from the literal, we may seem to be approaching the realm of fantasy and science fiction. But in fact, no specific discussion of setting in these genres is necessary. In fantastic fiction, setting may serve the functions we have been discussing and may range, like the settings of realistic fiction, from the neutral to the vital and essential. In short, what has been said here of setting in predominantly realistic fiction applies as well to nonrealistic fiction.

REVIEW OF FUNCTIONS

Let's now review what some of these functions are and the principal ways in which setting interacts with plot and character. The minimum of interaction is found in what we have called neutral setting. What neutral settings usually reflect is a low-level of interest on the part of the author in the kind of interaction we are now talking about. Whatever the writer who employs neutral settings may have to say about the human condition, it won't focus on the human being as situated in time and place. A good deal of commercial fiction treats setting in this way.

In some fiction, on the other hand, it seems that being situated in time and place—in an environment with a history—is what is most important and meaningful in the human condition. Such fiction may imply that external factors—factors of setting, essentially—determine largely, if not exclusively, who and what we are. Fiction that tends to imply this view of the human condition is often called naturalistic. Theodore Dreiser's *Sister Carrie* and *An American Tragedy* are generally numbered among the major works of American literary naturalism.

More subtle and complex patterns of interaction are possible. The work in which the central character is engaged in a direct or indirect struggle against the environment, especially against the spiritual setting, is one of the possibilities. *Jude the Obscure* is an especially powerful example of this pattern.

Another quite different pattern emerges in Henry James's *The Ambassadors*. Lambert Strether, the protagonist, travels from Woollett, Massachusetts to Paris. His mission, to simplify matters a bit, is to rescue the young American Chad Newsome from the snares of the wicked old city, which obviously functions here as a spiritual as much as a geographical setting. The central twist of the novel is that Strether finds himself captivated by Paris and is convinced that the supposedly wicked city has made Chad a finer person than he could ever have become in Woollett. But at a deeper level, we realize it is the aging Lambert Strether who has discovered in Paris possibilities in himself that he had never recognized back home. In short, James's novel is an ironic and exquisite examination of the possibility of setting as the occasion, even as the agent, of self-discovery and spiritual renewal in the individual.

In recent American fiction there has emerged yet another pattern—a work like Ann Beattie's *Falling in Place* may serve as an example. The action is set in a suburban area in Connecticut. Yet the details that establish this setting would fit equally well any suburban area anywhere in the United States. At first, this might seem very much like what we have called a neutral setting. What makes us hesitate about this classification is that the novel seems to give to the setting more attention than neutral setting calls for. Gradually we realize that the author has something to say about the setting: that it represents the homogenization of American society in our time. One suburb *is* very much like another, and the regional variations that delighted, fascinated, and absorbed the Cathers, Cables, and Jewetts of an earlier America are in the process of disappearing.

The setting in such a text is hardly neutral. Some of her readers and contemporaries will recognize in the picture painted by Beattie a profound truth about their own real-life "setting" or environment. But some may not. Some—I am of course speaking primarily about American readers—will find that the picture Beattie offers contradicts their own perceptions. How can such readers deal with a text like this?

Well, of course, they can reject it outright, but that seems an unpromising approach. Let's take it that we don't want to reject any work of fiction unless we have to—that is, let's give the text a chance to work.

In a case like this, there seem to me to be three possibilities to consider. One is to look very closely at the function of the setting in the text as a whole. It may be that a literal distortion of setting contributes in some valuable way to the overall effect of the work. Is it possible, for example, that we are dealing with an instance of setting as metaphor? Whatever our answer to this particular question, we must always place setting, like the other elements of fiction, in the context of the whole work.

Or it may be that on reflection I'll decide that my perceptions have been inadequate. I may, that is, be persuaded by the text to see the world rather as the author does. In short, the work of fiction may affect me in unexpected ways, open my eyes to possibilities of attitude and action that I've previously overlooked.

Or it may be that I do finally reject the author's perceptions and reaffirm my own. The key word here is *finally*. If there has been a true engagement of text and reader, the experience is one to be valued, even though I don't accept what the text is giving me. I've decided I value my perceptions over those of the author, but as I've been provoked to that decision, I've probably sharpened my perceptions. And that in itself is something to be grateful for.

SETTING AND THE WHOLE STORY: We have seen that setting may be the dominant element in a work of fiction. Still, setting never exists by itself. It is always part of an artistic whole and must be understood as such. Some readers turn to fiction out of a fascination with character. Certainly fiction can satisfy such an interest, but an interest in character divorced from the other elements of fiction is a psychological rather than a literary interest. Some readers may turn to fiction for what it can tell them of other times and other places. This too is a legitimate interest and one that fiction can satisfy. But an interest in setting divorced from the other elements of fiction is an historical or sociological, not a literary, interest. A literary interest will always concentrate on the whole work.

CHAPTER FOUR
POINT OF VIEW

INTRODUCTION: Twenty years ago, I wrote the following sentence: "Few topics have received more attention from serious modern critics of fiction than point of view"—not, I admit, a particularly memorable sentence. I mention it today because in the twenty years since it was first written, there has been a veritable explosion of interest in the study of fiction, part of a general renewal of interest in narrative, as distinguished from lyric or dramatic forms. This is in turn part of a major reorientation, if not an outright revolution, in literary criticism. And my point is that the sentence still seems to me essentially as accurate now as on the day it was written. Point of view (the terminology may vary) remains a central concern of critics of fiction. One might even conclude from a study of critical pronouncements on the subject that the choice of point of view is the most important single choice the writer makes.

At the same time, the average casual reader—the kind of reader for whom fiction is a form of escape to be indulged in during one's leisure time—hardly seems aware of the issues involved in the choice of point of view. It is scarcely an exaggeration to say that the very term *point of view* is either unfamiliar to or misunderstood by the average nonprofessional, nonscholarly reader of fiction.

All the same, it seems clear that, whether consciously or not, the average unreflective reader is affected by point of view and whether or not it is the most important choice the writer must make, it is one to which careful attention must be paid. If this is so, then we had first better be sure that we know what we mean by point of view. One of the problems we face is that the expression *point of view* has several meanings other than the limited, technical one it has in the critical analysis of fiction. In fact, my awareness of this problem has led me from time to time to give serious consideration to finding another term to use for this topic. But I finally decided that since this is the term most commonly used, I would only be inviting confusion by introducing another.

DEFINING POINT OF VIEW

WHAT POINT OF VIEW IS NOT: It may be best to begin by distinguishing the meaning of point of view in literary terms from other meanings that may be assigned to the same phrase. If you are asked for your point of view on a subject, what do you understand by the request? Chances are, you conclude you're being asked to express your opinions or attitudes. This is one sense of point of view; it is not, however, the sense we have primarily in mind when we speak of point of view in fiction.

AN ANALOGY: Let's try an analogy. Let's compare point of view in fiction with point of view in purely perceptual or physical terms. If I stand directly in front of you, I can't see your shoulder blades. If I am to see your shoulder blades, one of us has to move. That is, I have to look at you from another point of view. In short, from any single physical point of view, there are some things I can see and some things I can't.

THE EYEWITNESS: Now let's imagine that an accident has occurred: two cars have collided. There are four eyewitnesses to the accident. An investigating officer questions the witnesses. He also questions the drivers of the two cars and a passenger who was in one of the cars. He questions seven people in all. And he finds that he has seven different accounts of what happened.

Let's make clear that nobody is lying. Each person is telling the truth to the best of his or her ability. Why then don't their stories coincide in all details? Because each is speaking from a different point of view.

When we say this, we mean in part that each person saw the accident from a different point of view in physical terms. One witness was on one side of the street, another on the other side, and so on. But we mean a little more. A witness who just happened to be passing by is not involved in the accident in the same way that the drivers are. Relatively speaking, the passerby's involvement is rather remote. The passenger, though certainly more immediately involved than the passerby, is not involved in the same way as the driver.

Whose story is likely to be most reliable? Well, the drivers were most directly involved, but their involvement may make them unreliable because they can't be entirely objective. A passerby would probably be more objective but might have observed less. The passenger's account would be useful but limited.

In short, no single account could be expected to tell the whole story, yet each will provide something that the others lack. The only account that could give the whole story is God's, and that isn't likely to be available.

THE AUTHOR'S POWER: In fiction, however, something like a godlike view of things can be available. The author's relation to the world created in the work of fiction is, after all, similar to God's relation to the created universe. That is, the author is the ultimate source of being of every person, place, thing, and event in the work. The author knows all there is to know about these creatures of the imagination. But the author must decide whether it is desirable to exploit this special knowledge and must decide, in short, on the point of view most appropriate to the story being told.

POSSIBLE POINTS OF VIEW

FIRST PERSON OR THIRD PERSON?: A story may be told from the inside or the outside. When we speak of a story told from the inside, we mean a story told by one of the participants or characters in the story. Stories told from the inside are generally spoken of as examples of first-person narration, since the narrator naturally uses the first-person pronoun "I" in references to himself or herself. Stories told from the outside by a usually nameless narrator who may be more or less closely identified with the author are usually spoken of as examples of third-person narration. The term (rather an awkward one perhaps) is derived from the fact that the narrator refers to all of the characers in the story in the third person: "he," "she," "they," proper name (Mrs. Bennet), or descriptive phrase or title ("the young woman," "the count").

OMNISCIENT OR LIMITED?: The distinction between first-person and third-person narration is often made and has its uses. But a distinction based merely on grammatical form is likely to be superficial. (We shall see, however, that this apparently superficial distinction may have significant implications.) A still more basic distinction is that between omniscient and limited narration.

THE OMNISCIENT NARRATOR: Authors who choose to exploit their godlike knowledge of the fictional universe they have created will employ the omniscient narrator. Within the framework of the fictional text, the omniscient narrator simply knows everything. This narrator can at will enter the mind of any character and tell the reader directly what the character is thinking. The omniscient narrator is, as a rule, also omnipresent. That is, our narrator can at one moment be in the heart of the city; at the next, in a remote spot in the country. The narrator can move with a similar freedom through time, taking us from the present in one sentence to the past in the next. And the only motive required for the omniscient narrator's moves from mind to mind, from place to place, from time to time is the impulse to tell the story as well as possible.

Thackeray's *Vanity Fair* is one of the classic examples in the English language of the use of the omniscient narrator. Thackeray carries this technique very far indeed (too far perhaps for the tastes of some modern readers), for his narrator not only knows everything about the people and events in the story, he knows as well a good deal about the world in general and frequently interrupts the narrative proper for the purpose of introducing—sometimes seriously, sometimes ironically—bits of moral or philosophical reflection. Such interruptions, we may point out, are no necessary part of the technique of omniscient narration and are largely avoided by twentieth-century authors who employ omniscient narration. For the mark of the omniscient narrator is not philosophizing but the faculty of knowing all.

The omniscient technique is essentially a third-person technique. Even when, as in *Vanity Fair*, the narrator is a nonparticipant in the action and refers to himself in the first person, the actual participants in the action remain in the third person.

Earlier, you'll remember, we said that a third-person narrator may be more or less closely identified with the author. In the paragraphs just above, on the other hand, we have carefully maintained a distinction between author and narrator. The point is that the identification between narrator and author can never be absolute. The narrator is the being, ultimately fictional, who tells the story. The author is the creator of the narrator. To put it another way, the author is the person who has decided that on this occasion a third-person narrator is called for; the same author may on another occasion employ a first-person narrator. The author Herman Melville employs a first-person narrator in "Bartleby the Scrivener" and a third-person omniscient narrator in *Billy Budd, Sailor*.

THE ADVANTAGES OF OMNISCIENCE: In a sense, omniscient narration is the most natural of all narrative techniques. After all, the author, the figure behind the narrator, is—with regard to the work— omniscient. And because omniscient narration is in this sense the most natural form, it will be for many authors the most comfortable form.

In addition, omniscient narration is a highly flexible technique. As we have suggested, in omniscient narration there are virtually no limits to what the narrator can tell us. The narrator can always give us just what the story demands and need have no other concern.

THE DISADVANTAGES OF OMNISCIENCE: Although omniscient narration is in one sense a particularly natural technique it is in another sense an essentially unnatural one. After all, in life there are no omniscient people. The narrator who knows all and tells as much as serves the purpose is a convention of fiction. For those who regard "naturalness" in fiction as desirable, omniscience is not always the most desirable choice.

Furthermore, the very flexibility of omniscient narration, while certainly a virtue in itself, can present problems. In the hands of an insufficiently disciplined writer, omniscient narration can tend to looseness and incoherence; the technique does not in itself impose discipline on the writer.

LIMITED NARRATION: The alternative to the omniscient narrator is the limited narrator. As has been implied, limited narration is always artificial, because there are in truth no limits to an author's knowledge of the work the author has created. Still, art is in part a matter of artifice, and the artifice of limited narration offers a number of advantages to the writer of fiction. It also has its disadvantages, and we shall examine some of them as well.

THE NARRATOR: The limited narrator is simply a narrator who doesn't know everything. Such a narrator may appear in stories told from the inside (first-person narration) and in stories told from the outside (third-person narration). It is when we turn to the limited narrator that some of the most powerful possibilities inherent in choice of point of view begin to become clear. In a sense, the omniscient narrator *is* a point of view but *has* none. Able to observe the action from all possible angles but not personally involved in that action, the omniscient narrator simply sees things as they are—at least, as they are in the imaginary world of the story.

PROTAGONIST AS NARRATOR: The omniscient narrator, like God, has no point of view. But characters, like people, have points of view. And when the story is told by one of the characters, rather than by an omniscient narrator who serenely and disinterestedly views the action from above, then we may clearly say that the story is told from a particular point of view.

The story may be told, for instance, by the protagonist, or main character. In that case, it's told from that character's point of view. We see only what the protagonist sees, and we see it only as the protagonist sees it.

The use of the protagonist as narrator has certain obvious advantages. It corresponds very closely to the reader's experience of life, for each of us is in a way the protagonist of a first-person story. Like the protagonist-narrator, we know ourselves from the inside and other people only from the outside. I know my own thoughts directly. The thoughts and feelings of others I must infer from their words and actions. Therefore, the use of the protagonist as narrator, telling his or her own story in the first person, has the advantage of immediacy and the sense of life.

A further advantage of this method is that it can make a positive contribution to the overall unity of the story. Bound to include in the story only what the narrator can be expected to know, the author is thus provided with a valuable principle of selection that can assist in avoiding the looseness sometimes associated with omniscient narration.

The advantages of telling the story from the point of view of the protagonist suggest some of the disadvantages connected with the method. What in some stories may be a source of immediacy, intensity, and unity can be simply an unfortunate restriction in others. The author may be frustrated at being able to include in the story only what a character may be expected to know. If the point of view has been unwisely chosen, the author may resort excessively to tricks for introducing additional information. Examples of this would include an overly heavy reliance on letters or telephone calls, and mechanical conversations between the protagonist-narrator and secondary characters to convey information. All of these devices are legitimate in themselves, but excessive reliance on them becomes too obviously a mechanical solution to a technical problem, distracting our attention from the story to the author's difficulties in writing it.

There are also problems arising from the fact that in a story told by the protagonist we are in a sense locked within the mind of the protagonist. This is not in itself a flaw, but it suggests that the method may not be suitable for all subjects. For instance, moral judgment of the protagonist is difficult to handle in a story told by the protagonist unless the reader can be convinced that the protagonist is more given than most of us to self-analysis and self-evaluation. Even Henry James, one of the masters of point of view, doesn't quite succeed in his story "The Aspern Papers" in solving the problem of how to incorporate a moral attitude toward the protagonist in a story told by the protagonist. In this generally remarkable story, we are left with the sense that on this occasion James has tried to make first-person point of view do more than it can.

Yet first-person point of view has many triumphs to hold up against this partial failure. The well-known stories of Edgar Allan Poe, such classic short stories as Sherwood Anderson's "I Want To Know Why" and Eudora Welty's "Why I Live at the Post Office," and such masterpieces of the novel as Charles Dickens's *Great Expectations* attest to the range and flexibility of this technique.

A question that may arise in connection with first-person point of view is "To whom is the narrator speaking?" At times there may be an answer. In Poe's "A Cask of Amontillado," for instance, it seems that the narrator is speaking to his confessor some fifty years after the main events of the story have occurred; he is, in fact, most probably making a deathbed confession. This lends an irony to the story, because of his obvious lack of repentance the confession is unlikely to lead to the narrator's salvation. More commonly though, the first-person narrator is not speaking to so well-defined a listener as this. In the case of Poe's "Fall of the House of Usher," for instance, it's impossible to determine to whom or from what vantage point (e.g., how long after the events themselves) the narrator is speaking. In fact, it's often true that first-person narration must be accepted as a useful artifice, chosen for its effectiveness, rather than for its probability. To whom, in most cases, is the first-person narrator speaking? To the reader of the story.

PROTAGONIST AS VIEWPOINT CHARACTER: Closely related to the point of view we have been discussing is what is most often called third-person limited narration. In this technique the story is told from the outside by a narrator who, like the omniscient narrator, is not a character in the story being narrated. But in third-person limited narration the narrator is not omniscient. In third-person limited narration, as the term is primarily understood, the narrator knows all there is to know about one character. This includes the inner life—the thoughts and feelings—of the character. Beyond that the narrator knows only what this one character knows. The controlling point of view is that of this character, who is therefore referred to by critics as the viewpoint character.

The viewpoint character may be the protagonist, in which case the method is very close to the first-person technique discussed above. The principal difference is that in the first-person technique, narrator and protagonist are one and the same; whereas in the third-person technique they remain clearly distinguished from one another.

This difference has important implications. The narrator in a third-person limited story is always more or less detached from the viewpoint character. This detachment presents an opportunity for kinds of irony, evaluation, and interpretation not easily manageable in first-person narration. Consider, for instance, the following brief passage from Henry James's novel *The Ambassadors*. "Strether" is Lambert Strether, the novel's protagonist and viewpoint character:

> Many things came over him, and one of them was that he should presently know whether he had been shallow or sharp. Another was that the balcony in question didn't somehow show as a convenience easy to surrender. Poor Strether had at this very

moment to recognize the truth that, wherever one paused in Paris, the imagination, before one could stop it, reacted.

There is nothing in the first two sentences that could not, with the necessary changes in grammatical form, be included in a story told in the first person. But at the word "Poor" in the third sentence, narrator and viewpoint character part company. "Poor" is the narrator's comment on the viewpoint character, and this kind of comment is, of course, impossible in first-person narration.

A further distinction between the two types of point of view may be mentioned. In third-person narration the viewpoint character will generally share in the fallibility that is part of the human condition. On the other hand, we take the narrator to be completely reliable as to facts and also as to judgments and interpretations. When the narrator refers to Strether as "Poor Strether," it doesn't occur to us to question the narrator's judgment. Although the narrator in James's novel is not omniscient—he doesn't "know" everything—he is totally reliable. What he does say may be trusted implicitly.

First-person narration may, on the other hand, exploit a rather different possibility. Often we take the first-person narrator to be completely reliable, or at least we don't consciously question that reliability. In *Great Expectations*, when Pip, the narrator and protagonist, accuses himself of having become a snob, we don't question his judgment. In part, this is because the judgment seems borne out by the facts the narrator has given us; that is, our acceptance of the judgment is based on our prior acceptance of the narrator's reliability as to the facts. Also, we understand the narrator's vantage point as contributing to his reliability: an older, more mature, more experienced Pip is passing judgment on his younger, immature, inexperienced self. Beyond this, we might say that everything in the text implies that this is the right way to see the narrator.

It is, however, a different matter when in Poe's "Tell-Tale Heart" the narrator assures us of his sanity. Most of us conclude that the narrator in this case is quite wrong. A number of factors contribute to this difference, and it would take us too far afield to go into them here. Readers are, however, invited to pursue this question themselves. At any rate, Poe's story demonstrates that first-person narration opens up the fascinating, if at first disorienting, possibility of unreliable narration. In a story like this one we as readers must finally determine what is to be regarded as true.

Apart from these important distinctions, first-person and third-person limited narration have much in common and share many of the same advantages and disadvantages. The author is restricted to what might convincingly be known by the narrator in first-person narration and by the viewpoint character in third-person limited narration, and this can be either a valuable discipline or a frustrating restriction, depending on the temperament and talent of the author and on the nature of the material.

MINOR CHARACTER VIEWPOINT: Although our remarks to this point have assumed that the narrator in first-person narration and the viewpoint character in third-person narration is the protagonist, this need not be the case. Either role may be assumed by characters of lesser importance. Minor character viewpoint obviously has many of the same strengths and drawbacks as major character viewpoint, whether first person or third person. There is the additional problem that telling the story from the point of view of a character other than the protagonist seems to require a special kind of justification. If a story is at all interesting, the protagonist's point of view should be interesting, since the story is the protagonist's story. But what makes a minor character's point of view interesting? Well, first of all, the minor character employed as narrator or viewpoint character isn't likely to be as minor as all that. Dr. Watson, narrator of the Sherlock Holmes stories, isn't the protagonist of those stories, but he is a character of very considerable importance. More to the point is that Watson's relation to the great detective is fascinating in itself. Much is added to the impact of the stories by the fact that we see the exploits of Holmes, the hero, through the admiring but not precisely dazzled eyes of his friend and chronicler. Watson's point of view permits us to see facets of the situation that we would otherwise miss, just as in *The Great Gatsby* the narrator's ambiguous relation to the fashionable and sophisticated society makes him an especially perceptive and valuable commentator on the action of that novel.

OBJECTIVE VIEWPOINT: An extreme instance of limited narration occurs when the narrator is not permitted to know directly the thoughts of any of the characters. This narrator can observe and report only what becomes external in word and action. The technique is often referred to as objective or sometimes as dramatic narration (and occasionally as objective-dramatic). Ernest Hemingway is a writer who in stories like "The Killers" explored the possibilities of the objective viewpoint. Dashiell Hammett's novel *The Maltese Falcon* is a striking and powerfully sustained example of the objective viewpoint. A consequence of Hammett's determined refusal to send his narrator inside the characters is that this is one detective novel in which the detective is in many ways the most mysterious character.

Given the right kind of subject, as in "The Killers" and *The Maltese Falcon*, the objective viewpoint can have great force. Its insistence on letting surfaces speak for themselves can create a powerful sense of honesty and integrity. On the other hand, its refusal to deal directly with the inner life is finally a serious limitation, since it is thereby obviously unsuited to many of the subjects great writers of fiction have considered most important.

COMBINATIONS: The basic points of view in fiction, then, are the omniscient and the limited. The limited may involve either first-person or third-person narration; the narrator or viewpoint character may be either the protagonist or a secondary character; an extreme form of the limited point of view is objective narration.

Now, these different narrative techniques may appear in combination in the same story. In fact, a work of fiction that is as a whole an example of omniscient narration will usually include all or most of the other points of view as well. That is, at some point in the narrative the omniscient narrator will simply describe externals and will therefore temporarily assume the objective point of view. At another moment the narrator will present a scene to us from the viewpoint of one of the characters and will therefore employ third-person limited narration.

MULTIPLE VIEWPOINTS: Not to be confused with a combination of different viewpoints is the use of multiple viewpoints, which is actually a particular application of the limited point of view. An important example is William Faulkner's novel *As I Lay Dying*. Part by part, Faulkner's consistent use of the limited point of view is clear. At any given moment in the novel, the action is being witnessed from the point of view of a single character. We see only what that character sees and only as that character sees it. But the novel as a whole contains no less than sixteen viewpoint characters. We see the action from the point of view of each one in turn.

I call your attention to the word *see* in the sentence you've just read. Have you noticed how often the analogy to vision, to seeing, has been stressed in this chapter? It's not too long ago, in fact, that we were talking about looking at shoulder blades. The very concept of point of view is ultimately visual, and this is true of all uses of the phrase, not just the literary one.

THE NARRATIVE VOICE: But as we've developed the points of this chapter we've talked not only in terms of point of view but also in terms of narration. And narrating, I think we can agree, isn't a matter of seeing; it's a matter of saying. To narrate is to *tell* a story, not just to witness one. It's time, then, that we shifted our attention a bit from seeing to saying or, if you prefer, from focalization to vocalization. We've been talking, we might say, about the narrative eye. We must now consider the narrative voice.

In the rest of this chapter, we shall not be considering all of the many topics that might come under the heading of voice in fiction. We'll concentrate rather on a few areas in which focalization and vocalization are closely related. And we'll be concerned especially with passages that represent some form of limited narration. Keep in mind, though, that, as we said above, such passages may occur in texts that taken as a whole would be regarded as examples of omniscient narration.

RELATION BETWEEN NARRATOR AND VIEWPOINT CHARACTER VOICES: The first topic we'll consider is that of the relation between the voice of the narrator and the voice of the viewpoint character. As the term *viewpoint character* suggests, this is an issue that arises especially in stories or passages dominated by third-person limited narration. In first-person narration, where there is no distinction between narrator and viewpoint character, this issue should dissolve.

Well, maybe it should, but there are texts in which the matter becomes a bit more complicated. Occasionally, there appears a discrepancy between the qualities of the narrator's voice as we hear that voice in the narrative passages and as we hear it in passages of dialogue. The hard-boiled detective novels of Raymond Chandler, for instance, are narrated by Philip Marlowe, the private detective who is also their protagonist. When Marlowe speaks to the other characters in dialogue, his speech is vernacular, slangy, and tough. On the other hand, when he speaks to the reader as narrator he sounds much more literate and even literary, given to often striking, sometimes startling figures of speech. He seems to speak in two voices.

The question for the reader is, what am I to make of this perceived discrepancy? Is Chandler simply being careless? Well, it's a possibility, of course, but it's not the sort of judgment a good reader makes without considering other possibilities first. That is, we prefer those readings that make such difficulties seem purposeful and significant. Only when we are satisfied that no such reading of a passage is possible do we conclude that the writer has failed.

In the case of Chandler, it seems that we are meant to see that Marlowe operates on two levels. His voice when he speaks to others is that of a tough guy in a tough world. But when he speaks to himself, and to us, we hear the sensitive romantic idealist he keeps hidden from others.

The point here is not to push a particular interpretation of the works of Raymond Chandler but simply to indicate that the relation between the voice of the viewpoint character and that of the narrator can be a matter of some complexity even when the two voices are, from another angle, the same.

THIRD-PERSON NARRATION: The possibility of differences between the voice of the narrator and that of the viewpoint character becomes perhaps more evident as we move from first- to third-person narration. But it is probably more appropriate to think of a range of possibilities from the very similar to the very different.

EXAMPLE FROM JAMES: Third-person limited narration is the choice commonly preferred by Henry James, as in *The Ambassadors,* quoted earlier in this chapter. It is characteristic of James's fiction in this mode that the voice of the narrator and the voice of the viewpoint character have much in common. Here's a paragraph from his short story "Paste":

> But Arthur Prime, it was clear, had already thought the ques-
> tion over and found the answer easy. "If they had been worth
> anything to speak of she would long ago have sold them. My
> father and she had unfortunately never been in a position to keep
> any considerable value locked up." And while his companion
> took in the obvious force of this he went on with a flourish just
> marked enough not to escape her: "If they're worth anything at
> all—why, you're only the more welcome to them."

There may be a difference in degree of subtlety between the two voices, as in the narrator's "flourish just marked enough not to escape her." But in a real sense Arthur and the narrator speak the same language. They belong clearly to the same milieu.

EXAMPLE FROM CRANE: The relation between narrator's voice and viewpoint character's voice is very different in much of the work of James's friend, admirer, and younger contemporary Stephen Crane. For the most part, Henry Fleming is the viewpoint character in Crane's masterpiece *The Red Badge of Courage.* Here is the narrator's voice:

> The observant regiment, standing at rest in the roadway,
> whooped at once, and entered whole-souled upon the side of the
> maiden. The men became so engrossed in this affair that they
> entirely ceased to remember their own large war. They jeered the
> piratical private, and called attention to various defects in his
> personal appearance; and they were wildly enthusiastic in support
> of the young girl.

And here is the voice of Henry Fleming:

'Well, . . . lots of good-a-'nough men have thought they was going to do great things before the fight, but when the time come they skedaddled.'

And here is the voice of the narrator narrating Henry's thoughts:

The youth was in a little trance of astonishment. So they were at last going to fight. On the morrow, perhaps, there would be a battle, and he would be in it. For a time he was obliged to labor to make himself believe. He could not accept with assurance an omen that he was about to mingle in one of those great affairs of the earth.

The thoughts in this paragraph are the thoughts of Henry. But the voice is the voice of the narrator. Only in the second sentence of the paragraph do we find language that sounds at all like the Henry of the dialogue passage quoted above.

The question, then, is not only who sees but who speaks, and what is the relationship between them? Do narrator and viewpoint character speak pretty much the same language, as is commonly the case in James, or do they differ sharply, as in the examples from Crane? And is some kind of attitude, moral or otherwise, implied in either case? By making us see Henry as relatively inarticulate, does Crane remove him to some degree from the glare of our judgment, prepare us to see him later as not in the full sense a responsible agent, not to be condemned when he runs away or perhaps to be praised when he leads the charge? And does James, by contrast, in making Arthur Prime all but measure up to the narrator's very level of articulateness, suggest that this is a character who can be held responsible for whatever happens to him?

Again, it's not my intention to argue for a preferred interpretation. I merely want to suggest some of the ways in which the narrator's vocalizations can, perhaps significantly, complicate our relation to the viewpoint character.

In reading *The Red Badge of Courage*, we are strongly aware of the distinctive voice of Crane's narrator. It is, of course, also possible for the narrative voice to be suppressed. In some of Hemingway's stories—"A Clean, Well-Lighted Place" comes to mind—there are sustained passages consisting entirely of dialogue, without even the minimal but apparently not obligatory "he said." Such passages may be regarded as examples of what some critics have called by the apparently paradoxical name of non-narrated narrative. The distance from the character maintained by Crane's narrator and the subtle moral shadings established by James's, give way to the illusion of immediacy. The implication seems to be the refusal on Hemingway's part to offer a narrator as guide to our reactions.

But dialogue still suggests the realm of the public. As we've already seen, the narrator can put us directly in touch with the character's thoughts and feelings, with what we often call the inner life. Yet the question of voice remains. In the Crane example the narrator has, we may say, organized Henry's thoughts into a style consistent with the nondialogue portions of the rest of the text. An alternate possibility is to suppress the narrator's voice here as well. The inner life is then given as it may be before a deliberate narrator starts to organize it. The classic example would be Molly Bloom's soliloquy, the final passage of James Joyce's *Ulysses*. Also found in this direction is the stream of consciousness represented elsewhere in the same novel:

> Looking down he saw flapping strongly, wheeling between the gaunt quay walls, gulls. Rough weather outside. If I threw myself down? Reuben J's son must have swallowed a good bellyful of that sewage. One and eightpence too much. Hhhhm. It's the droll way he comes out with the things. Knows how to tell a story too.

We move here from an initial perception of the viewpoint character in the relatively straightforward first sentence to a free play of sensations, reflections, memories, and grunts. The attempt is apparently to give us a representation of the process or stream of consciousness of Leopold Bloom, the viewpoint character.

THE FREE INDIRECT STYLE: From the ironic distance established by Crane's narrator to the self-effacement in this passage of Joyce's, the range is wide. And somewhere within that range, we find a quality of narrative voice that has in recent days received an abundant share of critical attention. I refer to what has come to be called the free indirect style. Let's start with an example.

> Yes, being *the* Slade's widow was a dullish business after that. In living up to such a husband all her faculties had been engaged; now she had only her daughter to live up to, for the son who seemed to have inherited his father's gifts had died suddenly in boyhood. She had fought through that agony because her husband was there, to be helped and to help; now, after the father's death, the thought of the boy had become unbearable. There was nothing left but to mother her daughter; and dear Jenny was such a perfect daughter that she needed no excessive mothering.

The passage is from Edith Wharton's "Roman Fever." We are being given the thoughts of Mrs. Slade, who is the viewpoint character in the passage. The question is whose voice is speaking and with what implications?

I want to focus on the words "dear Jenny was such a perfect daughter." The story as a whole is an example of third-person omniscient narration, moving easily from the mind of Mrs. Slade to that of her companion. As is usually the case in third-person narration, whether omniscient or limited, we accept the reliability, indeed the infallibility, of the narrator. The question that arises is what role is the narrator playing in the words I've just quoted?

Note the difference between the words as quoted and this version: "Dear Jenny is such a perfect daughter." This sounds like Mrs. Slade's thoughts in Mrs. Slade's words. It is to Mrs. Slade, her mother, that Jenny is "dear" and "perfect." And she is these things now; that is, the present tense confirms our notion that we have here a mother's present thoughts about her daughter in the mother's own words.

Now try this version: "She regarded Jenny, who was dear to her, as a perfect daughter." The thoughts are pretty much the same thoughts. Jenny is still dear and perfect. But "she regarded" establishes a distance between narrator and character. The thoughts are Mrs. Slade's and *not* the narrator's; it is to Mrs. Slade and *not* to the narrator that Jenny is dear and perfect.

Now, look again at the words Edith Wharton actually wrote. The context may tell us that the thoughts are Mrs. Slade's thoughts, but the language in itself is more ambiguous. We don't quite have Mrs. Slade's own words, but neither do we have the marks of narrative distance. The principal unambiguous mark of the narrator's presence is "was," a past tense that makes us aware that we are still dealing with third-person narration. Yet in the framework of third-person narration, Jenny is described as "dear" and "perfect," words that make sense coming from a mother, rather than from a supposedly infallible third-person narrator.

What happens, then, in free indirect style is that the voice of the narrator and that of the characer seem almost to merge. Out of this arises a kind of ambiguity—who is finally the source of what is being said?—that the writer can exploit in a number of different ways. In the passage quoted, for instance, an ironic transfer of authority seems to occur. It's as though the narrator is endorsing the mother's doting, while at the same time making sure we know who is doing the doting. In fact, we are being prepared here for the story's ironic final twist.

Once the free indirect style has been called to our attention, we quickly realize that examples of it abound in fiction. The passage we've been looking at and commenting on merely suggests a few of the possibilities of this technique.

POINT OF VIEW AND MEANING: Treated in isolation from the other elements of fiction, point of view may seem to the less experienced reader a narrowly technical concern. After all, it may be objected, it's the story that counts, not the point of view from which it's told.

But this objection is unsound, for story and point of view are not truly distinct entities. Would the same story, told from another point of view, be just as good? The truth seems to be that you can't tell the same story from another point of view. Change the point of view, and you change the story.

Imagine "The Killers" or *The Maltese Falcon* retold as a firstperson story with Ole or Sam Spade as narrator. Would they still be the same stories? Surely not. Nor would *The Great Gatsby* be the same story if it were told by an uninvolved omniscient narrator rather than by the sensitive and sympathetic Nick.

POINT OF VIEW AND CHOICE: We return once again to the theme of choice. You have been invited throughout this book to regard the work of fiction as a complex but coherent form determined by a series of choices made by the author in the process of composition. In truth, the author is always omniscient. But the author may choose to tell the story through a narrator who is not omniscient. And this choice, as much as any other made by the author, has formal, moral, and philosophical significance. It is not "merely a matter of technique" (whatever that might mean) but part of the meaning of fiction.

CHAPTER FIVE
STYLE AND TONE

INTRODUCTION: Although each of the topics discussed earlier in this book concerned us specifically as an element of fiction, no one of them is relevant only to fiction. Much of what we say of plot in fiction, for instance, is also applicable to plot in drama.

At the same time, no one of these topics is applicable to all forms of literature. There is, for instance, no plot, in the usual sense of the term, in a lyric poem or essay.

The topics we shall discuss in this chapter, on the other hand, are qualities of all literary forms—one might almost say of all uses of language. Every literary work at least possesses the qualities of style and tone. What we shall be concerned with in this chapter is the particular relevance of style and tone to our understanding of fiction.

STYLE

RELATION OF STYLE AND TONE: As we shall see in the course of this chapter, the role of style in a work of fiction is an important and complex one. But none of the effects we may attribute to style is more important than its contribution to the establishment of tone. In this relationship, we may regard style as the means, and tone as the end. We shall first examine the nature of the means.

MEANING OF STYLE: We must first be aware that the word *style* has a number of meanings. When scholars speak of the "Attic style," for instance, they are speaking of a literary tendency that has especially flourished in some periods but may be discovered in any period. On the other hand, there are period styles that are characteristic of one historical period and are not to be found to any significant extent in any other.

We are more concerned with individual style, the use of language by one writer, but we would be wise to remember that the full understanding of an individual writer's style may involve seeing the style in the context of the general style of the period and of recurrent literary tendencies. The style of the great English essayist Sir Francis Bacon, for instance, may best be examined and appreciated for its own qualities by one who can recognize its relation to the Attic style and to English prose of the later sixteenth and earlier seventeenth centuries in general.

Even when we have agreed that our principal concern is with individual style, some ambiguities remain. If, as occasionally happens, the complaint is made that a writer has no style, style seems to mean a generally desirable literary quality that some writers have and others do not. On the other hand, if we hear that Theodore Dreiser or James T. Farrell is an unsatisfactory stylist, we may conclude that all writers have style but not all styles are satisfactory.

Finally, if a critic undertakes an analysis of, say, Henry James's style, it may turn out that evaluation is all but impossible. After all, Henry James's style is undoubtedly Henry James's style. That is, style may simply mean a writer's characteristic way of using language. It is in this sense that all writers have style. And who can say that one writer's style (say, Dreiser's) is inferior to another's (say, James's)? Isn't it possible, after all, that one style in this sense is never better or worse than another but only different from it?

STYLE AND STANDARDS: The usual purposes of literary analysis demand that we be able to describe and evaluate the material we are examining—first of all, to describe. It is then desirable that we isolate at once the particular qualities of a writer's style without attempting to judge either the individual qualities or the style as a whole. With a writer like Dreiser, for example, we must try to understand his style on its own terms, without being in too great a hurry to impose on it our notions of the kind of style we prefer. We should not condemn Dreiser simply because he is not Henry James. Neither, if our tastes tend in a different direction, should we condemn Henry James for not being Dreiser. A large part of this chapter will be devoted to suggesting methods and vocabulary that should be helpful in analyzing a writer's style on its own terms.

But in the discussion of literature, we almost always come at last to the act of judgment. A number of standards for evaluating style have been suggested at one time or other. For some critics, economy is the supreme virtue; the writer must on no account use more words than are necessary. We may assent to this standard in a general way and still ask, "Necessary to what?" Other critics prize concreteness above all else; yet we must recognize that the degree of concreteness in a given writer's work may quite properly be determined by the overall design of that work.

What we need, then, is a standard that will serve as a fairly useful guide and still remain flexible enough to prevent our condemning a writer for not achieving what was in fact quite properly never attempted. The only standard I have ever found that meets these conditions is appropriateness; the style must be appropriate. If I am asked, "Appropriate to what?" I can only answer, "To everything else in the work." Style like every element of fiction, must ultimately be judged by its contributions to the artistic whole.

STYLE IS THE MAN: A traditional assertion of literary criticism has been: "The style is the man." In this traditional form, it may have a vaguely sexist ring—the style, let us remember, is also the woman—but this assertion is relevant to our consideration of style in fiction. Part of our experience of the total work of fiction is our sense of the author, our awareness of and response to the qualities of the author's mind and personality. And authors reveal these qualities nowhere more clearly than in their styles. The choice of words and the arrangement of words into larger units such as the phrase, the sentence, and the paragraph are not merely mechanical processes. A writer's style can reveal to us a way of perceiving experience and of organizing those perceptions into some sort of meaningful pattern. The differences in style between a Dreiser and a James, the more subtle differences between a James and a Wharton, are ultimately differences of mind and personality.

But it may be objected that the style of many writers, including the authors of many best-selling novels and of stories in widely read magazines, is nothing more than a matter of formula. How can a formula reveal an individual writer's qualities of mind and personality? But doesn't one writer's willing submission to formula reveal such qualities as well as another writer's resistance to formula? It remains true, of course, that a formulaic style rewards analysis less than does an authentically individual one. It is also occasionally the case that what strikes us at first as a formulaic style may, on closer examination, prove an interesting and expressive variation on the formula. The hard-boiled style of much American crime fiction is in itself little more than a formula and by now a rather tired one. But writers like Dashiell Hammett and Raymond Chandler have, at their best, made the formula a point of departure for impressive achievements of personal style.

STYLE AND UNITY: Unity of style in itself may be sufficient to give total unity to a lyric poem or a familiar essay, for in these forms the direct expression of a mind or personality is what the work is all about. But although fiction may express the mind and personality of its author, it does so indirectly. Making a plot, after all, and creating characters who both serve the plot and take on an independent existence of their own—the work of the fiction writer—are not exactly direct forms of self-expression. Style alone, therefore, is not sufficient to unify a work of fiction in which the other elements form no coherent relationship with one another. But style can work in cooperation with the other elements of fiction to produce a final unity. A loosely, though not incoherently, plotted novel like *The Sun Also Rises* benefits especially from the unity of style that reflects the controlling mind and personality of Ernest Hemingway.

THE ELEMENTS OF STYLE: Qualities of mind and personality revealed through style can also contribute greatly to our sense of the significance of the work. For example, many admirers of Jane Austen would agree that the world she depicts in her novels is a limited one, and yet they would argue that Austen herself is one of our major novelists. What distinguishes her work, for many, is precisely the sense of the fine intelligence and tough-minded sympathy of the author, qualities conveyed not through her subject matter but through her style.

On the one hand, then, style is the expression through a characteristic use of language of the author's mind and personality, often lending unity and significance to the work of fiction. On the other hand, and perhaps at a more mundane level, style is simply everything the author does with words, including the way the author arranges words into such larger units as sentences. We shall consider this topic under three headings: diction, imagery, and syntax.

DICTION

Diction means simply the author's choice of words. Our purpose in the analysis of diction is to recognize the choices the author has made and to infer when possible the reasons for which the choices have been made. Obviously, a knowledge of the options available to the author— which may include knowledge of the literary conventions of the author's period, say, or for that matter of literary conventions in general— will be useful in this undertaking. But even when we don't bring to the text a scholar's familiarity with such matters, we may be able to discern something of a pattern of choices.

Our assumption in the analysis of diction is that any choice may be significant and that the sum of choices in a whole work will certainly be so. As we turn our attention from the diction of a brief passage to that of an entire story or novel, we look for the author's guiding principles of selection and for hints of a pattern in the choices the author has made. We may on occasion undertake the same kind of investigation of the diction in the total body of a writer's work (the term *oeuvre* is sometimes employed to refer to this total body of work).

We then seek to discover what kind of choices the writer habitually makes and for what reasons.

DENOTATION AND CONNOTATION: The analysis of diction almost invariably leads to some considerations of denotation and connotation in the writer's language. The terms *denotation* and *connotation* have technical meanings in some contexts, mostly philosophical. But in discussions of literature, a word's denotation is normally simply its dictionary meaning, while its connotations are the suggestions and associations aroused by it. Language more generally tends to the denotative insofar as it emphasizes statement and to the connotative insofar as it emphasizes suggestion. A number of different words may have essentially the same denotation while differing significantly in their connotations. Is a man who reveals the shady business practices of his associates an "informant" or a "stool pigeon"? Is a man who is slow to change his mind determined, stubborn, or pigheaded? The differences among these terms, and they are certainly considerable, are largely matters of connotation. Some suggest admiration, some express contempt, and some are neutrally descriptive. You decide which is which. And of course, the possible shadings of connotation can be far more subtle than this.

A question we can start with in any particular analysis is, to what extent does the writer exploit the suggestive powers of language based on the connotations of words? Some writers, we will discover, choose or evolve a diction in which there is a minimum of suggestion or connotation and maximum of statement or denotation. Other writers seem to make suggestiveness their major principle of selection. The suggestiveness or lack of it in a given writer's diction will, however, always be relative. A language absolutely without connotation is impossible in fiction, and for that matter in ordinary discourse, and a language absolutely without denotation is no language at all.

DENOTATION—AN EXAMPLE FROM SWIFT: The diction of *Gulliver's Travels* by Jonathan Swift may seem to take little advantage of the suggestive powers of language. Here, for instance, is a passage describing the emperor of Lilliput:

> He is taller, by almost the breadth of my nail, than any of his court, which alone is enough to strike an awe into the beholders. His features are strong and masculine, with an Austrian lip and arched nose, his complexion olive, his countenance erect, his body and limbs well proportioned, all his motions graceful, and his deportment majestic.

This is about as close to pure denotation as we may expect a passage of prose fiction to come. The meaning of the passage, at least at one level, is little more than the sum total of the dictionary meanings of the words that make it up.

Why should a writer so purify his language of the suggestiveness that other writers strain to achieve? There are a number of probable reasons for the choices Swift makes in this passage.

Swift's choices are no doubt influenced in part by the period style, the norm of prose in English in the first half of the eighteenth century. We shall not enter here into a dissertation on this subject beyond noting that the development of a plain style, suited to the purposes of the scientific and rational, and resistant (or so it was hoped) to the superstitious and fanatical, is one of the principal tendencies in the period.

Even to a reader familiar with the period style, though, Swift's diction seems unusually pure of connotation. Let us note as a partial explanation that Swift's plot, involving at this point Gulliver's adventures in a land whose inhabitants are approximately one-twelfth the size of normal human beings, is itself sufficiently fantastic. Perhaps Swift felt that the greatest sobriety of style was necessary if the audience was to accept the fantasy, or at least that fantastic subject matter and sober prose style might create a pleasing contrast.

Further, *Gulliver's Travels* employs a first-person narrator. The plainness of the diction may therefore be seen as a reflection of the narrator's character. Lemuel Gulliver, in spite of his fantastic adventures, remains a rather unimaginative man.

Finally, Swift, even by the standards of his time, was deeply suspicious, indeed fearful, of the irrational elements in human character, and this attitude is reflected throughout *Gulliver's Travels*. The suggestiveness of language is not based primarily on reason, and the writer who exploits it is therefore appealing to the nonrational, if not the irrational, in human beings. Such an appeal would violate Swift's purpose in his satirical narrative, that is, encouraging his readers to act more reasonably.

The emphasis on the denotative powers of language in Swift's diction, then, seems based on the demands of the work and the qualities of Swift's personality, both of which reflect qualities of the period. But in spite of this emphasis on the time, the man, and the work, the connotative is not entirely absent from the passage. The quality of unimaginativeness in the character of Gulliver has been suggested, as we noted above. And if we place the passage in a larger context—that is, the whole account of Gulliver's first voyage—the combination of the regal and the petty in the emperor's appearance takes on satirical implications. Again, the language of fiction is never entirely denotative, even in the hands of a master of statement like Jonathan Swift.

We might mention before moving on that there was a further level of implication for Swift's first readers, who recognized in the text a political allegory involving satirical comments on political figures and issues of the day. For the nonscholarly modern reader, this is the stuff of footnotes, but again it suggests the impossibility, even if such were a desirable thing, of a purely denotative style in fiction.

DENOTATION—AN EXAMPLE FROM HAMMETT: Yet strongly denotative styles continue to exist in the twentieth century as in the eighteenth. We spoke before of the hard-boiled style. Here's an example, from one of the masters:

> Spade's thick fingers made a cigarette with deliberate care, sifting a measured quantity of tan flakes down into curved paper, spreading the flakes so that they lay equal at the ends with a slight depression in the middle, thumbs rolling the paper's inner edge down and up under the outer edge as forefingers pressed it over, thumb and fingers sliding to the paper cylinder's ends to hold it even while tongue licked the flap, left forefinger and thumb pinching their end while right forefinger and thumb smoothed the damp seam, right forefinger and thumb twisting their end and lifting the other to Spade's mouth.

Now you know how to roll your own cigarette. The passage from Dashiell Hammett's *Maltese Falcon* has the denotative clarity of good directions. Again, we might ask why a writer would choose such a flatly denotative style.

Part of the explanation lies in plot and in the principle of pleasing contrast I referred to in connection with Swift. Sam Spade has just been informed of his partner's murder. As the plot takes a sudden and dramatic leap forward, the style slows things down and flattens them.

Character is also involved. Spade is the kind of man who responds to news like this coolly. The coolness is implied in the unemotional language as well as in the apparent triviality of the action. Spade's competence, his ability to get the job done, is also implied in his mastery of the technique of rolling a cigarette.

The traits of Sam Spade that we've found implicit in Hammett's stylistic choices are traits Hammett seems to value throughout his *oeuvre.* That is, style seems once again to be reflecting the mind and personality of the author. And our repetition of words like "implied" and "implicit" remind us that style is never purely denotative.

CONNOTATION—AN EXAMPLE FROM POE: In spite of their shared emphasis on the denotative aspects of language, Swift and Hammett are very different writers. Edgar Allan Poe is a writer who differs from both of them in his emphasis on the connotative, suggestive powers of language. Here is the first sentence of his famous story, "The Fall of the House of Usher."

> During the whole of a dull, dark, and soundless day in the autumn of the year, when the clouds hung oppressively low in the heavens, I had been passing alone, on horseback, through a singularly dreary tract of country, and at length found myself, as the shades of evening drew on, within view of the melancholy House of Usher.

The diction here is characterized by the vagueness of denotative reference. Just how low is "oppressively low"? What precisely does a "dreary tract of country" look like? And how can a house be "melancholy," since the dictionary meaning of the word has to do with a human emotional state?

In short, Poe is choosing his words primarily for their connotative power. His method is as legitimate as Swift's and as suited to the demands of his story and his temperament.

A COMBINATION—AN EXAMPLE FROM THACKERAY: Swift and Poe come close to the practical extremes of statement and suggestion in diction. Few writers of fiction go so far in either direction. A diction relying on connotation more than that of Swift and more on denotation than that of Poe is closer to the norm. In the following passage from Thackeray's *Vanity Fair*, connotations reinforce the general drift of denotations. Mr. Osborne and his daughters are about to go to dinner:

> The obedient bell in the lower regions began ringing the announcement of the meal. The tolling over, the head of the family thrust his hands into the great tail-pockets of his great blue coat with brass buttons, and without waiting for a further announcement, strode downstairs alone, scowling over his shoulder at the four females.

Thackeray's control of connotations contributes to our sense of Mr. Osborne's dictatorial nature. He is referred to not by name or as "father" but as "the head of the family"; the phrase suggests authority.

By speaking of "the four females," rather than "his four daughters," Thackeray avoids all suggestion of familial warmth and intimacy. And it is, of course, significant that the bell is not only punctual but "obedient."

In discussing the passages from Swift, Hammett, and Poe, we concentrated on the significance of denotation and connotation for the work as a whole. The passage from Thackeray exhibits a controlled suggestiveness working within an individual passage to provide insight into character and into the quality of the situation. These selections and our discussions of them should give some indication of the importance of the author's choice of words and of the power that rests in the suggestiveness of words.

The dividing line between diction and imagery is difficult to draw because images are made of words, and a single word can be an image. Furthermore, the terms *image* and *imagery*, like most widely used critical terms, take on different meanings in different contexts. In our discussion an image is the evocation through words of a sensory experience; imagery is simply the collection of images in the entire work or in any significant part of the work.

IMAGERY

LITERAL IMAGES: Images may be either literal or figurative. A literal image involves no necessary change or extension in the meaning of the words. Swift's reference to the emperor of Lilliput's "arched nose" is an example of a literal image.

Since fiction deals with people, places, and things, and their relationships in action, it must depend heavily on literal imagery. A basic function of literal imagery is simply to satisfy the reader's demand for specific, concrete detail and the desire to know how things look, sound, smell, taste, or feel. It contributes to the vivid representation of experience that we expect from the best fiction.

RECURRENT IMAGES: While remaining literal in each individual instance, images may make an added contribution to the overall design of a story if they appear frequently in the text. In William Faulkner's short story "Dry September" there are a number of images of dryness. For the most part, the individual images are perfectly literal. It has not rained for a long time, and the land is parched and dry. Yet by their frequent recurrence, the images take on a suggestive power, arousing associations with barrenness, sterility, impotence, and frustration, all of which are relevant to the story's meaning.

Recurrent imagery may consist of a number of repetitions of the same image or the frequent occurrence of images that, while not identical, all relate to a single theme. The images may be entirely literal or may be a mixture of the literal and figurative.

FIGURATIVE IMAGES: Figurative images are sometimes called tropes or, more commonly, figures of speech. An image is figurative when it must be understood in some sense other than the literal. Robert Burns's "My love is like a red, red rose" is an example of a figurative image, since the love (whether the reference is to the emotion, to the woman who is the object of the emotion, or, as I suspect, to both at once) cannot in any clear way be literally like a rose.

The line from Burns is an example of a particular kind of figurative image called a simile. A simile is an explicit comparison of markedly dissimilar objects or entities (love and roses), involving the use of such comparative words as *like* or *as*. A bolder figure is metaphor, in which, because the comparison remains implicit, the statement seems to assert an identification. If Burns had said, "My love is a rose," this would have been metaphor.

The frequency with which a writer resorts to figurative imagery is an important quality of style. Jonathan Swift and Ernest Hemingway are two writers, obviously dissimilar in many ways, who are alike in that they make sparing use of figurative imagery. Thomas Wolfe, on the other hand, is an example of a writer of fiction in whose style figurative imagery is a major element. The stylistic austerity of Swift and Hemingway reflects the austerity of their views of human experience. Wolfe's highly figurative style, involving the frequent uniting of dissimilar objects and sensations, suggests an exuberant and uncritical openness to a wide range of experience.

Figurative imagery used recurrently is likely to be significant. In Stephen Crane's *Red Badge of Courage* men are frequently compared to brute animals. The recurrence of this kind of imagery suggests a skepticism, important to the novel's meaning, about the supposed uniqueness of the human being's place in the universe. It seems to be implied that humans are essentially animals, driven blindly, like other animals, by their instincts and that they are not the rational, moral, spiritual beings, acting on the basis of "values" and "principles," that they like to imagine themselves.

In the best fiction, figurative imagery is not merely ornamental but is an integral part of the total meaning of the work. The rarity of figurative language in Hemingway, like its abundance in Wolfe, is impressive because of its appropriateness to the whole structure of the work.

The particular pattern of recurrent imagery in *The Red Badge of Courage* is an important key to that novel's meaning. We may well be pleased by vividness and originality in imagery, but the ultimate question is always, "What does it contribute to the whole work?"

SYMBOLS: A symbol is basically a kind of image, differing from other images in the use to which it is put. Because symbolism often proves a stumbling block for inexperienced readers, we shall approach the subject indirectly.

We are all familiar with one kind of symbolism, the one we call language. Words function as symbols of their referents, the things they refer to. The word *tree* symbolizes a class of material objects. But as a symbolic system, language is limited. We don't have a name for everything. Even in relatively simple discourse on familiar topics we must resort frequently to modifiers. Note how many modifiers I have used in the preceding sentence. I had to attach "relatively simple" to "discourse" because we don't have a single name—a symbol—for the thing I had in mind.

But even with the help of modifiers, there are many things that cannot be talked about—as you know if an experience has ever left you speechless. For we have by no means succeeded in embodying all of human experience in language.

Now, a literary symbol may well be regarded as simply the author's attempt to name those many areas of human experience that ordinary language, literal or figurative, is inadequate to deal with. This is all we mean by the more formal definitions of symbolism that we may fashion on occasion. It is in this attempt that the symbol, while evoking a concrete, objective reality, also suggests an additional "level of meaning" beyond that reality. The writer's use of symbols is continuous with the process of language that we know.

AN EXAMPLE FROM MELVILLE: Herman Melville's *Moby Dick* is widely regarded as one of the greatest symbolic novels. In reading a work like *Moby Dick*, it is important to remember that the white whale does not "stand for" something that can be neatly stated in other words. Rather, Moby Dick (the whale, not the book) names a whole range of experience that had never been named before and for which we still have no name other than the one Melville gave it.

Moby Dick is an instance of a novel essentially symbolic in its design. The symbol may, of course, play a less central role in a given work of fiction. The green light at the end of the dock in Fitzgerald's *Great Gatsby* is an example of a symbol employed to extend the significance of the novel's nonsymbolic action.

As this discussion indicates, the symbol, although related to the image, may transcend the boundaries of "style"—in the more limited sense in which we have been using the word—to become the major structural principle of the work. But if we remind ourselves that style is the reflection of the author's way of perceiving and of organizing perceptions, we can see that even a symbol of the magnitude of Melville's whale remains related to the concept of style.

SYNTAX

To move from the symbolic resonance of the white whale to the frequency of subordinate clauses may seem a crashing anticlimax. Yet syntax, or the way the writer constructs sentences, is as essential an element of style as any we have been discussing.

In analyzing a writer's syntax, we concern ourselves with such matters as the characteristic length of sentences, the proportion of simple to complex sentences, and so on. These matters are by no means as trivial as they may at first appear. If the sentences of Henry James are characteristically longer and more complicated in structure than those of Ernest Hemingway, this may well reflect each writer's personal vision of life. For James the perception of experience is a matter of the close observation of fine distinctions; the embodiment of such a vision in prose requires a certain complexity of syntax. To rewrite a story by James in the syntax of Hemingway (or the other way around) would be to change the nature and meaning of the experience.

STYLE AND FIRST-PERSON NARRATION: A special problem in the analysis of style arises in the work of fiction that employs first-person narration. Is the style with which the reader is confronted properly to be considered that of the author or of the narrator? Is *The Adventures of Huckleberry Finn* written in the style of Mark Twain or Huck Finn? Is *Lolita* written in the style of Vladimir Nabokov or of Humbert Humbert?

The answer varies from text to text. In a work like *Great Expectations*, there is little to distinguish the style of the narrator Pip from what we know from other texts as the style of the author Charles Dickens. Edgar Allan Poe, who favored first-person narration, varied the style to suit the narrator: compare the narrator's styles in stories like "The Fall of the House of Usher," "The Purloined Letter," and "William Wilson." Yet most readers also feel that the style in an Edgar Allan Poe story is always unmistakably that of Edgar Allan Poe. Mark Twain in *Huckleberry Finn* convinces us that we hear throughout the voice of an uneducated and essentially uncivilized adolescent boy.

The general principle that seems applicable is easy to formulate if not always so easy to apply. The style of a work of fiction narrated in the first person may be thought of as the style of the author so adapted as to reflect the character of the narrator. The degree of adaptation may vary; William Faulkner doesn't find it necessary to abandon Faulknerian syntax and vocabulary when the narrator is supposed to be a young boy. And our sense of the degree of adaptation involved in a particular work will, of course, be more or less sure according to the number of other works by the same author with which we are familiar. The reader who has read most of Mark Twain will have a fairly good notion of where Mark Twain leaves off and Huckleberry Finn begins.

As a general rule, moreover, we may expect an author to have more than a little in common with the character the author chooses as narrator. The boxing trainer who narrates Hemingway's story "Fifty Grand" would never have been used as a narrator by Henry James, simply because James could never have felt his way into the mind of a character so different from himself. And if Huckleberry Finn is younger and more naive than Mark Twain, he pretty consistently arrives by instinct at the kind of perceptions and insights that had become Twain's by long experience in observing human nature. We may expect, then, that there will be a consistency between the style of the author and the style of the narrator he is likely to employ.

TONE

We have, for the most part, been considering style as a self-contained topic. But earlier in this chapter it was pointed out that one of the most important functions of a writer's style is its contribution to the establishment of tone in the work of fiction.

DEFINING TONE: What do we mean by tone in fiction? Perhaps the meaning of this term will become clearer if we think first of a more familiar sense of tone—that is, the sense in which we speak of tone of voice. We recognize that in spoken English the same words may add up to a compliment or an insult. Consider, for instance, the phrase "nice work." Say this in one tone of voice, and it's praise; say it in another, and it's the opposite.

By tone, then, we mean the expression of attitudes. In spoken language it is primarily the intonation of voice (just how one says "nice work") that reveals the tone and thereby suggests the attitude. In written language, including the language of fiction, tone is primarily a quality of style that reveals the attitude of the narrator (and by inference, the author) toward subject and audience.

AN EXAMPLE FROM O'CONNOR: Let us consider, for instance, the subject of the loss of religious faith. For the religious person, or for people capable, whatever their personal beliefs, of taking religious beliefs seriously, this is certainly an important subject. With this in mind, examine the following sentence: "My pal Mick Dowling started losing his faith very early, when he wasn't more than eighteen."

The sentence quoted is the first sentence of the story "Anchors" by Frank O'Connor. If we look closely at this sentence, we see that it suggests that the loss of religious faith is a common experience; what is singular about Mick is that he went through this experience rather earlier than most. In short, the subject of the loss of religious faith, which certainly might lend itself to intensely serious treatment, is in this story not treated very seriously at all. Rather, it is treated as something, like baldness or matrimony, that happens to most men sooner or later.

The expression in the story of this rather casual attitude toward the loss of faith is a matter of tone. And the tone is in turn dependent on matters of style. "My pal Mick Dowling started losing his faith very early. . . ." The suggestion is clearly that there is a time for losing one's faith; it is bound to come sooner or later, and in Mick's case it comes sooner. Consider this version: "Mick Dowling was eighteen years old when he lost his faith in God." The colloquial "pal" is gone. The word order is changed; the loss of faith, instead of being tucked away in the middle of the sentence is at the end, a more emphatic position. The phrase "in God" makes explicit what in the original is left implicit. As a result, although the same event is referred to in both versions, my rewrite makes the loss of faith—which the whole sentence is constructed to point out—a weightier matter. The same facts done in a slightly different style produces a different tone. O'Connor's style describes this potentially shattering experience with an attitude and tone of easy relaxed tolerance.

But O'Connor's sentence establishes an attitude, not only toward the subject but also toward the reader. "Look here," it seems to say, "we're sophisticated adults. We know that religious faith is something one inevitably loses; the only question is when. At any rate, we're not going to get excited about it, are we?"

Not all readers will be able to accept this attitude. For some, it will simply be too flippant on a subject they take very seriously. Others will accept it easily, because they confuse it with their own attitude (not O'Connor's) of contempt for religious faith. Still others will accept O'Connor's attitude because it is in fact their own. And some will provisionally accept O'Connor's attitude, not because it is their own or because they confuse it with their own but because they see it as an attitude that, however limited, may yet reveal something valuable about the subject.

Whether one accepts or rejects an author's attitude, that attitude is revealed to us in fiction primarily through tone. And tone is dependent on style, that is, on what the writer does with language.

UNDERSTATEMENT: In particular, the sentence from O'Connor's story is an example of understatement. That is, O'Connor treats his subject less seriously, less heavily than writers traditionally have done. Understatement has been much favored by modern authors. It seems particularly suited to the distrust of absolutes that is commonplace in our time. The author who understates does not commit himself very firmly to anything. The particular tack of O'Connor's opening sentence is that it does not take a stand for or against religious faith or the loss of it. Faith and apostasy are presented as elements of human experience, neutral in themselves but equally available to the writer of fiction.

Understatement may be, as it often is in the fiction of Frank O'Connor, a way of avoiding commitments. (I do not mean this as a condemnation.) On the other hand, the use of understatement may be a way of calling on the reader to react with the full power of moral imagination. The austere, nonfigurative style of Ernest Hemingway is a version of understatement, but its effect is quite different from the understatement of O'Connor. When in his story "A Way You'll Never Be," Hemingway describes without the slightest expression of moral outrage the proper technique of rape, his purpose is certainly not to suggest that rape is a trivial matter. On the contrary, he forces us to see that in a brutal world a deadening of the moral sense seems necessary to survival, and that this may be the ultimate indictment of the brutality we have come, in our time, to take for granted. Understatement, then, becomes a means of arousing in the reader the complete moral response of which Hemingway's characters are no longer capable.

IRONY: Closely related to understatement, but more clearly focused, is the tone critics usually refer to as "irony." Irony as a matter of tone consists of a discrepancy between what is stated and what is suggested. Irony in its crudest form becomes sarcasm. We say the opposite of what we mean: the words "nice work" function as a way of saying, "You've really botched it this time."

The writer of fiction occasionally resorts to sarcasm, but, if he is a writer of any distinction, the irony is likely to be more subtle. In Gulliver's Travels, the king of Brobdingnag, the land of giants, is appalled at Gulliver's boastful account of the weapons of destruction devised by Europeans. "A strange effect of narrow principles and short views" is Gulliver's comment on the king's response. The reader is expected to see that the narrow principles and short views are really those of Gulliver and his fellow Europeans.

Jane Austen is a formidable ironist. Consider the first sentence of *Pride and Prejudice*: "It is a truth universally acknowledged that a single man in possession of a good fortune must be in want of a wife." I leave it to the reader to examine and reflect on the means by which Austen leads us to look with an ironic eye on that universal truth.

HYPERBOLE: The opposite of understatement is hyperbole, or exaggeration used for rhetorical effect. When at the beginning of *A Tale of Two Cities*, Dickens refers to the period of the French Revolution as "the best of times" and "the worst of times," he is indulging in hyperbole. The effect of hyperbole in this instance and in many others in fiction is a dramatic heightening. We know that no one time can truly be singled out as "best" and "worst," but we recognize that a given period may seem to be one or the other, or both simultaneously to those living through it.

THE MIDDLE STYLE: Hemingway is given to understatement and Dickens to hyperbole. Most writers, most of the time, fall somewhere in between, exemplifying what we may call the middle style. Properly handled, the middle style tends to create the impression of a fair and accurate picture of things as they are. Among modern American novels, Fitzgerald's *Great Gatsby* and Willa Cather's *My Antonia* repay study as examples of the middle style.

Because it avoids extremes, the middle style may seem to represent some sort of ideal. But the avoidance of extremes is not necessarily the highest of literary values. Jean Cocteau once defined genius as "the art of knowing how far to go too far." We should sorely miss the work of such "extremists" as Hemingway, Faulkner, Dickens, Dostoevsky, Celine, Bernanos, Graham Greene, and Flannery O'Connor among others.

SENTIMENTALITY: Failures in tone occur when the attitude of the author seems somehow inadequate to the material presented. Once again the verdict of failure should not be arrived at too hastily. Such failures, when they do occur, often take the form of sentimentality, the attempt to impose on the material a greater emotional burden than it can comfortably bear. The death of Little Nell in *The Old Curiosity Shop* by Dickens is a classic example of sentimentality. Because Nell is a purely artificial figure, more an idealized doll than a child, the emotion Dickens tries to stir up at her death is excessive. Bret Harte and O. Henry are two American writers often accused of sentimentality.

Although sentimentality usually involves some exaggeration, it should not be confused with legitimate uses of hyperbole. The line between legitimate and illegitimate exaggeration is, however, not always clear, and intelligent and informed readers may sometimes disagree in their evaluation of particular passages. Moreover, a writer who, like Dickens, is capable of using hyperbole very effectively, is more likely to slip into sentimentality than a writer whose style is characterized by understatement. The appropriate question for the reader is whether exaggeration is justified by context or by its function in the work as a whole.

INHIBITION: Another kind of failure of tone is inhibition, the author's failure to give due emotional weight to his or her material. This is a problem more likely to arise in the work of a writer who, like Hemingway, is generally given to understatement. In fact, Hemingway at his worst and, even more, his many imitators sometimes understate their way to a kind of death, or at any rate inhibition, of feeling.

Another kind of inhibition can occur in the work of a scrupulous stylist like Henry James; the elaboration of style in bad work by James sometimes leaves feeling behind. Again, the fault that occurs occasionally in James is more pronounced in his imitators such as James Gould Cozzens.

The term *minimalist* has recently been applied to such contemporary American writers as Raymond Carver, Ann Beattie, and Bobbie Ann Mason. Differing from one another in many important ways, these writers are linked by a quality of understatement in their style. It's not surprising, then, if their detractors sometimes accuse them of inhibition. Read them and decide for yourself.

CONCLUSION: The present chapter has only scratched the surface of the closely related topics of style and tone. Ultimately, only wide experience in reading fiction can make a reader a competent judge of style and tone. But to neglect these elements in analysis is to neglect the very sources of vitality in fiction.

CHAPTER SIX
STRUCTURE AND TECHNIQUE

INTRODUCTION: There are a number of elements of fiction that, while important in what they can contribute to the total work, are not easily classified under the general headings employed in the earlier chapters of this book. This chapter is concerned with those elements, introduced under the properly vague categories of structure and technique.

DESCRIPTION

DEFINING DESCRIPTION: The first of these miscellaneous elements we shall discuss is description. By description we mean the direct presentation of the qualities of a person, place, or thing. For some, description extends to the depiction of nonmaterial qualities, as when the author tells us directly of the moral nature of the character. In this chapter, however, description has a more limited meaning. It covers only the presentation of sensory qualities. The author is engaging in description in telling us that the character is a tall man, not in telling us that the character is a good man. Of course, it may well be a proper part of description to suggest moral and spiritual qualities as these may seem to be embodied in physical details.

AN EXAMPLE FROM DICKENS: Rather than discussing description further at this abstract level, let's look at an example of it. Here is a description of a character from Charles Dickens's *Bleak House*:

> Mr. Chadband is a large yellow man, with a fat smile, and a general appearance of having a good deal of train oil in his system. . . . Mr. Chadband moves softly and cumbrously, not unlike a bear who has been taught to walk upright. He is very much embarrassed about the arms, as if they were inconvenient to him, and he wanted to grovel; is very much in a perspiration about the head; and never speaks without first putting up his great hand, as delivering a token to his hearers that he is going to edify them.

This is brilliant description on many counts. It is, first of all, a vivid rendition of the physical presence of Mr. Chadband. But more than this, without departing explicitly from description, Dickens manages to tell us a good deal about the character of Mr. Chadband.

How does Dickens achieve his effects? We might note, for one thing, that there is nothing haphazard about Dickens's choice of details. He makes no effort to tell us everything about Mr. Chadband's appearance. Rather, he concentrates on the qualities of oiliness and awkwardness, suggesting through the visible physical details something, we suspect, of the inner qualities of the man. The awkwardness is suggested in images ("not unlike a bear," "as if . . . he wanted to grovel") indicating that Chadband barely qualifies as a human being. And this in turn lends irony to the detail of Chadband's raising his hand as if about to edify his hearers.

Let's take time to note that much of what we've just said depends on the reader's willingness to accept the idea of a rather close connection between outer appearance and inner quality. It is not, of course, necessarily the case that the connection be so close in real life. Once again, it's a matter of our recognizing and provisionally accepting (i.e., accepting on the understanding that some legitimate purpose is being served) a literary convention as convention.

SELECTION AND ARRANGEMENT: In the above passage of description, we see selection and arrangement in action. Effective description is not merely a matter of the writer's including all of the details that may come to mind. Rather, the writer must select those details most important and meaningful within the design of the whole and arrange them so that this design is realized.

Description in itself is a relatively static element in fiction. In the passage from Dickens, for instance, the story comes to a halt while Dickens presents Mr. Chadband to the reader. But notice that Dickens includes movement or the suggestion of it ("Mr. Chadband moves softly and cumbrously . . .") in his description and that the last detail he includes, that of the raising of the hand, is well chosen to lead us back into the action. Dickens makes us wait expectantly for the edifying words of Mr. Chadband.

The description of the emperor of Lilliput from *Gulliver's Travels*, quoted in the preceding chapter, is much less vivid, much more matter-of-fact, than Dickens's description of Chadband. The flatness of Swift's description is, of course, by no means an artistic flaw. Swift is employing, as we have noted, a first-person narrator, and what is illustrated to us in the passage is that passages of description in first-person narration may reveal as much about the narrator as about the person, place, or thing described. The very matter-of-factness with which Gulliver describes so remarkable a figure as the emperor suggests Gulliver's stable and unimaginative personality.

Successful description, then, is a matter of selection and arrangement based on the needs of the passage in itself and as part of the whole work. Although specifically concerned with physical details, good description may, with the reader's cooperation, suggest nonmaterial qualities as well. Although passages of description are of their nature relatively static, the better writers of fiction will as a rule avoid too sharp a sense of contrast between description and the dynamic development of the narrative.

We have been concentrating on the passage devoted primarily or exclusively to description. Often, of course, description is absorbed into the depiction of action. While this introduces additional complexities, most of what we've said here about the descriptive passage applies with a few modifications to description so absorbed into narrative.

NARRATIVE TECHNIQUE

PANORAMA AND SCENE: We turn now from description to some specific matters of narrative technique or ways of telling the story. A distinction whose usefulness has been demonstrated many times over in critical discussions of fiction is that between panorama and scene. While these terms may not be familiar to the general reader, the techniques themselves certainly are.

EXAMPLES FROM HAWTHORNE: Rather than beginning our discussion by trying to define these terms abstractly, let's look again at two passages we discussed in relation to plot in an earlier chapter. These are the opening passages of Hawthorne's stories "Young Goodman Brown" and "My Kinsman, Major Molineux." Here again is the passage from "Young Goodman Brown."

> Young Goodman Brown came forth at sunset into the street at Salem village; but put his head back, after crossing the threshold, to exchange a parting kiss with his young wife. And Faith, as the wife was aptly named, thrust her own pretty head into the street, letting the wind play with the pink ribbons of her cap while she called to Goodman Brown.

This is an example of what we mean by scenic presentation. It resembles in its manner of presentation a scene from a play or movie. The narrator brings us close to the particulars of action, in both the spatial and temporal sense. Spatially, we are close enough to observe the wind playing with Faith's pink ribbons. Temporally, there is a close relationship between the time it takes to read of these actions and the time it takes to perform them.

Now let us examine the opening of "My Kinsman, Major Molineux."

> After the kings of Great Britain had assumed the right of appointing the colonial governors, the measures of the latter seldom met with the ready and generous approbation, which had been paid to those of their predecessors, under the original charters. The people looked with most jealous scrutiny to the exercise of power, which did not emanate from themselves, and they usually rewarded their rulers with slender gratitude for the compliances, by which, in softening their instructions from beyond the sea, they had incurred the reprehension of those who gave them. The annals of Massachusetts will inform us, that of six governors, in the space of about forty years from the surrender of the old charter, under James II, two were imprisoned by a popular insurrection; a third, as Hutchinson inclines to believe, was driven from the province by the whizzing of a musketball; a fourth, in the opinion of the same historian, was hastened to his grave by continuous bickerings with the house of representatives; and the remaining two, as well as their successors, till the Revolution, were favored with few and brief intervals of peaceful sway.

The contrast between the panoramic technique employed here and the scenic technique of "Young Goodman Brown" should be clear. In "Young Goodman Brown," Hawthorne presents actions that take a few seconds to perform in a passage that takes a few seconds to read. In the passage from "My Kinsman, Major Molineux," he disposes of forty years (and six governors) in a single sentence. In "Brown," the physical setting is clearly presented and severely limited: the threshold of the home of Brown and his wife in Salem village. In "Molineux" the physical setting is highly generalized: the colonies in general and the Massachusetts Bay Colony in particular (that is, as specific as we get). The actions in "Brown" are individual; those in "Molineux" are representative. The passage from "Brown" has the directness of dramatic presentation; that from "Molineux" has the indirectness of narrative summary. In the passage from "Brown," we are hardly aware of the narrator (the phrase "aptly named" is the only strong reminder of his presence); in "Molineux" we are inevitably aware of the narrator as the one who selects, compresses, and summarizes the events of a long period of time, over a substantial expanse of space, into a single paragraph.

In this series of contrasts, we see the difference between scene and panorama. The difference is not always so clear-cut. A passage may be a good deal less generalized than the one we have been looking at from "My Kinsman, Major Molineux" and still be essentially panoramic. The essence of the scenic is its presentation of moment-by-moment action, often involving dialogue; in "Young Goodman Brown" the dialogue commences in the paragraph that comes after the one we've been dealing with. As a passage of narrative moves away from these qualities, it moves in the direction of panorama.

The choice between the panoramic and scenic technique is another of the important choices the writer of fiction must make. To understand something of what is involved in this choice, let's consider some of the ways in which the two techniques can be used. We should recognize at the outset that we shall usually find both techniques employed in a work of fiction and that the interplay of the one with the other is an important source of narrative rhythm. Some stories, for instance Hemingway's "The Killers," are entirely scenic. The entirely scenic novel is rare, but the contemporary American novelist William Gaddis has produced just that in *The Recognitions*, *JR*, and *Carpenter's Gothic*.

BEGINNINGS: As the examples from Hawthorne illustrate, the author may begin the story with a passage of either panorama or scene. Each method has its advantages. The scenic method is more likely to catch the reader's attention at once because of its concreteness and vividness of presentation. But the panoramic technique may offer the advantage of clarity. The panoramic opening of "My Kinsman, Major Molineux," for instance, lets the reader know exactly where we are in time and space and provides a context for the specific actions to follow, actions for the most part presented scenically. Knowledge of the historical picture presented by Hawthorne (and, we might add, knowledge from the particular slant of the narrator) is essential to an understanding of what happens to Major Molineux.

Hawthorne could, of course, have found other ways to provide the reader with the essential historical information. He could have let much of it come out indirectly, through dialogue, say, as the story unfolds. But the method he chose is certainly more economical than any other. It allows him to get the necessary exposition out of the way at the beginning and to concentrate thereafter on the story's dramatic content. And it contributes to the narrative rhythm as it enters into a relationship of contrast with the scenic passages that follow.

A similar beginning, one that summarized, for instance, the history of devil worship in the colonies would have been, it seems to me, a disastrous choice for "Young Goodman Brown." The impact of this story depends to a great extent on our gradually increasing awareness of context and situation as the story unfolds. It also depends on our close involvement with the characters, particularly with Brown himself, an involvement that would be seriously compromised by the introduction at this point of the panoramic technique.

But Hawthorne demonstrates his mastery of the panoramic technique in this story and of narrative rhythm as well. The last paragraph of "Young Goodman Brown" is a devastating panorama of the remainder of Brown's life after that night in the forest. The sudden shift to the panoramic overview at this point in the story powerfully suggests the loss of meaning, variety, and vitality in the existence of young Goodman Brown.

The power that every reasonably sensitive reader must feel at the denouement of "Young Goodman Brown" suggests the kind of effects a writer can achieve through the interaction of panorama and scene. We'll now summarize some of the further functions this combination can serve.

ECONOMY: The panoramic technique tends to economy. It should be obvious that the material presented panoramically at the beginning of "My Kinsman, Major Molineux" could hardly be presented scenically within the confines of a single work of fiction. The material of the last paragraph of "Young Goodman Brown" could perhaps be presented scenically, but this would prevent the story from moving swiftly from climax to denouement. By shifting to panorama, Hawthorne avoids slipping into anticlimax, a severe drop in the reader's attention after the high point of interest has been reached. At any point in the story— beginning, middle, or end—the author may resort to panorama to present economically that which presented scenically would require an excessive amount of time and space in view of the story's overall design.

CHANGE OF PACE: Shifts from scene to panorama and back again can have the desirable effect of preventing monotony in the development of the story. We must recognize, of course, that the writer may be willing to risk some degree of monotony for the sake of some higher purpose, or that without departing from the scenic technique he may depend on devices other than change of pace (e.g., sheer interest in the characters or events of the story) to prevent monotony. As a general rule, however, monotony is something to be avoided, and the change of pace effected by the shift from scenic to panoramic is a good way of avoiding it.

EMPHASIS AND SUBORDINATION: It is the writer's job not only to present to us the events of the story, but also to indicate the relative importance to the story of those events. That is, the writer must emphasize what is of primary importance and subordinate what is of secondary importance. The writer has available a number of devices for emphasis and subordination. The traditional development from beginning through complication to climax, discussed under the heading of plot in an earlier chapter, is itself a means of emphasis: what is presented at a structurally pivotal moment will normally be perceived as important by the reader. But the proper use of scene and panorama can also contribute to emphasis and subordination. Material of secondary importance, like the historical background of "My Kinsman, Major Molineux," can be presented panoramically, reserving the scenic technique for moments of crucial importance.

That material is presented panoramically does not always mean, of course, that it is of secondary importance. The last paragraph of "Young Goodman Brown" is as important as any other in the story. But first, this is a panoramic paragraph in a story in which the scenic has hitherto been dominant, and any deviation from an established norm is at least potentially emphatic. This single paragraph also constitutes the denouement of the story; now we find out how it all turned out. The major structural position it holds, as well as the power of the human material it involves, more than offset the tendency to subordination that in a different context might be properly associated with the panoramic technique.

TRANSITION: Finally, panorama may serve a transitional function. While the crucial action in a story may be presented scenically, the author will sometimes take steps to bring the reader smoothly and without harmfully distracting confusion from one scene to another. In Anton Chekhov's story "The Lady with a Pet Dog," the memorable moments are presented scenically. But the story covers a rather long period of time, and its events occur in several different locales. The scenes, then, are widely separated in time and space. Chekhov could, of course, have simply juxtaposed the scenes of his story, but this would have produced a jarring effect, suitable for some stories but inappropriate to the demands of this particular story. Chekhov therefore uses panoramic passages as transitions from scene to scene.

The emphasis I have placed here on the benefits of combining scene and panorama should not lead the reader to infer that the exclusive use of one technique in a story is necessarily a flaw. I know of no examples of a purely panoramic story, but as we mentioned earlier, the entirely scenic story does exist and has had its triumphs. The exclusively scenic technique of "The Killers" is entirely appropriate to the peculiar kind of intensity, with its concentration on the present, that the story achieves. The novels of William Gaddis are fascinating for their un-usual narrative rhythm. Panoramic passages, placing characters and situations at a distance, tend thereby to lower narrative intensity, to introduce a note of relaxation in the narrative rhythm. The absence of such passages in Gaddis's novels (two of which, by the way, are quite long) contributes to a sustained narrative tension quite apart from the intrinsic qualities of the events of the plot.

DIALOGUE

The last element of fiction to be considered in this chapter is dia-logue, by which we mean the presentation in fiction of the actual words of characters speaking to each other. We shall consider both the qualities of dialogue and the functions it serves in fiction. Like imagery, dialogue is in part a means of satisfying a reader's demand for concrete-ness. In speaking of imagery, we observed that most readers want to know how things look, smell, taste, sound, and feel. We want to know this about the people in fiction, as well as about the places and things. Description can tell us a great deal about what a character looks like. It can also tell us something about how a character sounds: "He had a high, rasping voice." But the best way to find out how a character sounds is to listen to him talk. We were introduced to Dickens's Mr. Chadband in a paragraph quoted earlier in this chapter; now, let's listen to him talk.

> "My friends," says Mr. Chadband, "peace be on this house! On the master thereof, on the mistress thereof, on the young maid-ens, and on the young men! My friends, why do I wish for peace? What is peace? Is it war? No. Is it strife? No. Is it lovely, and gentle, and beautiful, and pleasant, and serene, and joyful? Oh, yes! Therefore, my friends, I wish for peace, upon you and upon yours."

The experience of hearing Mr. Chadband, the concreteness of the impression we receive, could not possibly be equaled by description, however precise. The demand for concreteness is satisfied only by Mr. Chadband's actual words.

DIALOGUE AND CHARACTER: In addition to satisfying our demand for concreteness, Mr. Chadband's speech serves another function: it tells us a good deal about Mr. Chadband. The empty rhetoric of his utterance, his apparent inability to wish someone well and let it go at that, his compulsive and patently insincere sermonizing all reflect the moral character of Chadband. Dialogue, then, can be an important means of revealing character.

The proposition that dialogue reveals character can be turned around to become character determines dialogue. For if we feel we know Mr. Chadband after hearing him, this implies that we assume some consistency between, on the one hand, what a man is and, on the other hand, what he says and how he says it. A consequence of this is that dialogue is often judged on the basis of its being or not being "in character." That is, we want to be convinced that the words put in a character's mouth are words he really would use. Dickens is especially adept among English writers of fiction at creating dialogue so closely related to character that we feel having once heard Mr. Chadband speak, we would recognize his voice immediately on hearing it again. This may be exceptional, but at least we usually may expect that no character in a story will speak in a way absolutely inconsistent with the traits of that character as we have come to know them, by whatever means.

NATURAL DIALOGUE: Along with the demand that dialogue should be in character, one often hears that it should be natural. The demand, I think, is a legitimate one, but we must be very sure that we know what we mean by it.

We must remember that fiction itself is not natural. Fiction imposes an artificial form on material—human experience—that is, at least as far as our perceptions can carry us, naturally formless. The essential artifice of fiction extends as much to dialogue as to anything else. When we demand natural dialogue, we must have in mind a naturalness that is somehow not inconsistent with a more fundamental artifice.

We must remember further that dialogue is always part of the larger whole, the story. A demand for naturalness that does not consider the design of the whole may turn out, upon inspection, to be a demand for incoherence.

Let's consider some of the things that will always be artificial about even the most "natural" dialogue in fiction.

DIALOGUE IS SELECTIVE: The distance between fictional dialogue and human speech may be more or less great, depending on the needs of the story and the stylistic preferences and practices of the author. But some distance there will always be. At the very least, fictional dialogue involves a process of selection from human speech. Ordinary human conversation, even the conversation of the most highly educated and articulate people, involves much that is rambling, irrelevant, and incoherent. How often do we find ourselves groping for words? How often do we, for all our groping, finally fail to say what we want to say? What can a tape recorder reveal to us about our habits of conversation? We might find that much of the time we sound like this: "It's, uh, you know, uh, uh, well, you know, sort of . . ."

In fact, the dialogue in the intensely scenic novels of William Gaddis that we mentioned earlier in this chapter comes closer than most to capturing the presence of aimless noise in human speech. His characters habitually utter strings of words like "yeah no yeah," strictly speaking, making no sense at all but producing a shock of recognition, at least in this reader. Yet even Gaddis is engaged in a highly artful selection and arrangement of the sounds we call language.

Characters in fiction, even realistic fiction, seldom sound the way you and I often sound in real life. Nor, to be honest, would we want them to. They don't because a process of selection is constantly underway, removing the grunts and hesitations, and this removal is obviously a departure from the natural.

Of course, characters in fiction do sometimes grope for words. But when this happens, you may be sure that the groping is at least as important as the words. That is, the author makes the speaker's inability to find the words he wants an indication of his character or emotional state or both. This does not in any way lead us to qualify what we've already said about the selective nature of fictional dialogue.

DIALOGUE AND STYLE: Another note of artifice in fictional dialogue is based on the relation between passages of dialogue and the author's style in general. The author must make the dialogue conform to the characters who speak it, but too great a discrepancy between the style of the dialogue passages and the style of the rest might produce a disconcerting effect that the author doesn't want. In such a case, the author will try to make sure that dialogue is not only consistent with the character but also with the author's overall style.

In practice this does not usually present much of a problem. The same mind, after all, is behind the dialogue and the characterization. It's true that Mr. Chadband's speech would be inconsistent with the style of Ernest Hemingway, but it's also true that a Mr. Chadband isn't likely to turn up in a Hemingway story. There are also some fictions in which it is precisely the multiplicity of voices that we hear or the complex relationship between the narrative voice and the voice of the characters that is a principal source of fascination. We noted in an earlier chapter that Stephen Crane's fiction often exploits the latter kind of tension, and the Russian critic Mikhail Bakhtin has held up

Rabelais and Dostoevsky, among others, as masters of a fiction based on a multiplicity of voices.

Does all of this mean that we must reject naturalness as a standard for dialogue? Not necessarily. But we may have to redefine naturalness.

A NEW MEANING OF NATURAL: Natural dialogue is dialogue that is like human speech. Well, what is human speech like? Let's take my speech, for example.

In general, my speech is a reflection of my personality and of the background and experiences that have shaped that personality. I am of Irish ancestry and was born and raised near Boston. In part, my speech exemplifies the accent associated with Bostonians in general and perhaps with the Boston Irish in particular. (I keep telling myself I've entirely lost that accent, and strangers keep asking me what part of Massachusetts I'm from.) I have been in the army, stationed in Georgia, and I resided for six years in Michigan. I now live in New York. In my travels, I've been exposed to the dialects of the various regions I've visited. I have, of course, also met people from other parts of the country and from other countries as well.

I am a college graduate and hold the M.A. and Ph.D. as well. I now teach courses in American literature, in composition, and in other subjects that come under the general heading of "college English." I am not fluent in any language other than English, but I have studied French, German, Latin, and Homeric Greek.

I suppose I come from a working-class background, but I admit the dividing lines between classes are not always clear to me. Neither of my parents—both of whom, by the way, were born in this country—finished high school, not an unusual situation for Irish-Americans of their generation, born right after the turn of the century. I was the third of four children.

This has been a random listing of some of the things in my life that might have affected my speech in such matters as vocabulary, pronunciation, grammar, syntax, and speech rhythm. The point is that my speech is obviously related to a number of other things. Any one of my readers could draw up a similar list; no doubt many of my readers' lists would differ in a number of ways from my own.

One thing most of us—obviously not all—have in common is that we are native speakers of American English as it is spoken in the twentieth century, and this is certainly a major shaping influence on our individual ways of using language.

Finally, my speech varies according to circumstances. I don't sound the same when talking to a large group as I do when talking to my wife or son; I don't sound the same when bored as I do when excited, and so on.

What all of this adds up to is that my speech, human speech, the model for the dialogue in a work of fiction, is one element in a large and complex pattern. I speak as I do partly because of my personality and experiences, partly because of the world I live in and the time I live in it, and partly because of the situation in which I find myself and to which my speech is a response.

If we want to demand that fictional dialogue should be natural, let's mean this: the relation of dialogue to personality, context (e.g., social position, education), and immediate situation (what's going on right now) in fiction should parallel the relation of speech to the same complex of elements in life. It should be added that the author's style adds to the context in fiction an element to which nothing in life exactly corresponds.

Putting it another way, dialogue in fiction should be natural to the world the author creates, not necessarily to the world in which author and reader really live.

NATURAL DIALOGUE—AN EXAMPLE FROM SWIFT: But let's be specific. Is the following speech from *Gulliver's Travels* natural? The king of Brobdingnag is talking to Lemuel Gulliver after Gulliver has given him an account of "the state of Europe."

> As for yourself . . . who have spent the greatest part of your life in travelling, I am well disposed to hope you may hitherto have escaped many vices of your country. But, from what I have gathered from your own relation, and the answers I have with much pains wringed and extorted from you, I cannot but conclude the bulk of your natives to be the most pernicious race of little odious vermin that nature ever suffered to crawl upon the surface of the earth.

Now, I don't know anybody who talks like that. I don't know anyone who's that eloquent, for one thing. But I have absolutely no hesitation in saying that in the context of the book of which it is a part, this is a perfectly natural way for the king of Brobdingnag to address Gulliver in this situation.

FURTHER FUNCTIONS OF DIALOGUE: We may note in conclusion three additional functions of dialogue. For purposes of simplicity, our examples will all be taken from "Young Goodman Brown."

DIALOGUE GIVES INFORMATION: Dialogue is one of the means by which the author conveys information to the reader. In "Young Goodman Brown," Brown insists that New Englanders are people of prayer and good work. The devil, in answering Brown, provides him and the reader with information that challenges that assertion and prepares us for what we'll find in the heart of the forest.

> 'I have a very general acquaintance here in New England. The deacons of many a church have drunk the communion wine with me; the selectmen of divers towns make me their chairman; and a majority of the Great and General Court are firm supporters of my interests. The governor and I, too—But these are state secrets.'

We must remember that information imparted by a character is never as reliable as information imparted directly to the reader by a reliable narrator. It seems that what the devil says is true because it is confirmed by the incidents of the plot. But a character may be misinformed or may be deliberately lying.

DIALOGUE REVEALS EMOTIONAL TENSIONS: Dialogue may reveal not only character but also the particular emotional tensions experienced by the character in a specific situation. The hesitations of Brown, the speeches in which he insists that he will go no farther with the devil, tell us a good deal about his inner emotional state. "There is my wife Faith," he says. "It would break her dear little heart; and I'd rather break my own." The speech indicates Brown's unwillingness, but it also indicates the weakness of his resolve. Simply by arguing with the devil, he is inviting rebuttal, and we are not surprised that he does not turn back.

DIALOGUE ADVANCES THE PLOT: The conflict that dominates the early portions of "Young Goodman Brown," as Brown carries on his argument with the devil, is developed primarily through dialogue. Each new speech advances the plot a step further. When Brown mentions his wife, we know he is nearing the end of his argument, and when the devil expresses concern for Brown's wife, we sense sinister overtones. The speeches, then, are by no means simply casual conversation, a way of filling a few pages. They are, rather, an integral part of the development of the conflict that is plot. And as dialogue leads us back to plot, we are reminded again that it is the story as a complex whole that must always be our concern.

CHAPTER SEVEN
MEANING AND VALUE

INTRODUCTION: In the course of the chapters that have brought us to this point, you may have noticed that two topics have had a way of turning up no matter what the stated topic of the chapter or part of a chapter. I refer to the topics of the meaning and value of fiction. It's now time to confront these two questions directly. In this chapter our principal concern will be meaning, but by this time you won't be surprised to find value—that is, questions of judgment, of the "good" and "bad" in fiction—turning up as well now and again.

CONNECTION BETWEEN FICTION AND MEANING: Comments on the meaning of a work of fiction, on the contribution of some feature or other to the story's meaning, and on what makes us perceive this or that element as meaningful have been turning up with some frequency as we have worked our way through the elements of fiction we've so far considered. But the question we now have to face is, what connection, if any, is there between fiction and meaning?

For fiction, as we all know, is not true. That's what makes it fiction. It is, for most of us much of the time, what the word means: a fiction is something that isn't true. Or there's fiction and there's fact, and fact is the stuff that's real.

And since fiction is not real, not true, how can it have any meaning? What possible significance can we find in a lot of unreal stories about unreal people?

THE ROLE OF ETYMOLOGY: Well, let's first clarify one thing. Etymologically—that is, according to the historical origins of the word—fiction does not mean something that is not true; it means something that is made. That is, the etymology suggests that the important thing about fiction is that it's the product of human work. And we shouldn't be too quick to say that any kind of human work is meaningless.

At the same time, we don't want to place too much emphasis on etymology. What a word may have meant long ago in another language (*fiction* comes from Latin) doesn't finally determine what the word means for us today and certainly doesn't necessarily tell us anything about that ever-growing body of texts we call fiction. If the claim that fiction has meaning is to be taken seriously, it must be grounded elsewhere.

THE "TRUTH" OR FACTS IN FICTION: One thing we obviously don't claim is that fiction is, tries to be, or claims to be "true" in the sense that a news story, a scholarly account of an historical event, a scientific report, or the latest rumor going around the classroom or the office is, tries to be, or claims to be true. Different as these phenomena are from one another, they have in common a certain kind of truth claim—that they can be verified, checked against the "objective" facts in the "real" situation, and, at least theoretically, finally established as true or false. Now, this is precisely the kind of claim that fiction does *not* make. And it is because fiction makes no such claim, that the question of whether fiction can have meaning in any acceptable sense of that word arises.

Complicating the picture somewhat is the practice writers of fiction occasionally follow of including in their fictional texts references to actual historical events and personages. In fact, on the day before typing these words, I read in the newspaper of a court decision affirming the right of a novelist to do exactly that, even when it involves making an actual living man a character in a novel and (I gather as I haven't read the book in question) painting the man—an archbishop, no less—in a less than flattering light.

Whatever the courts may have to say on the issue, writers have for a long time been incorporating the factual into their fictions. In Hawthorne's "Young Goodman Brown," to take an available example, the reference to Salem village is to an actual place, and our historical awareness of what was going on there in the late seventeenth century— I refer, of course, to the Salem witch trials—certainly contributes more than a little to the impact of the story. More, Goody Cloyse, who taught Goodman Brown his catechism and who participates in the demonic rites of the forest, is (or at any rate has the same name as) a woman who was hanged as a witch (an historical fact) during the period in which the action of the story takes place. In short, fiction may include a generous sprinkling of fact. We are not concerned here with the outer reaches of literary theory, but it might be mentioned that one of the most vexing questions for theoretically minded critics has been that of the dividing line between fiction and nonfiction.

As I've said, we don't aim here to settle such theoretical questions. It may suffice for our purposes if we say that we read a work as fiction if we don't finally care whether the text as a whole refers accurately to some situation outside the text. Whatever we want in fiction doesn't require it to make accurate factual statements about the external world.

MEANING IS NOT EXPLICIT: Putting it another way, the meaning of fiction, if any, is not referential. It's also the case, if we examine what critics say about the meaning of works of fiction, that that meaning is not explicit: it is not usually stated in so many words anywhere in the text. A short story or novel isn't usually presented to us as an example of some general moral or philosophical precept that's stated for our enlightenment and convenience at the beginning or the end.

There are, to be sure, stories in which the author-narrator does offer some sort of moral or philosophical summing up. Here are the closing sentences of Hawthorne's "The Birthmark":

> Yet, had Aylmer reached a profounder wisdom, he need not thus have flung away the happiness which would have woven his mortal life of the selfsame texture with the celestial. The momentary circumstance was too strong for him; he failed to look beyond the shadowy scope of time, and, living once for all in eternity, to find the perfect future in the present.

One's first reaction may be "How's that again?" But we certainly recognize the preachy tone, the voice of the narrator summing up and expaining Aylmer's failure—attempting through the exercise of his scientific knowledge to remove from his wife's cheek the birthmark he considers her only imperfection, he's been responsible for her death—and cautioning us against the same kind of error.

But you'll find, if you explore the extensive critical commentary Hawthorne's story has inspired, that sophisticated readers don't necessarily accept this passage as the last word on the story. Such readers are inclined to ask the question we have become accustomed to: how does this passage fit into the story as a whole? They at least feel that the rest of the text must be consulted to determine how to understand the highly abstract language of the passage I've quoted. In short, such readers seem by their practice to imply that even if we take this passage as the moral of the story, we can't look to the moral to find the meaning of the story. It may be more to the point to suggest that the story gives us the meaning of the moral.

By the way, if I understand the current state of scholarship on the matter, it seems that the morals traditionally appended to the *Fables* of Aesop, perhaps our most familiar examples of the story with a moral, are not part of the original but were added later on. Even these texts, at least in what we now suppose to be their original form, demanded that the audience arrive at the meaning through an act of interpretation.

READERS DO FIND FICTION MEANINGFUL: The meaning of a work of fiction, then, is not immediately forthcoming. Yet, as I've pointed out, in this book we've frequently talked about fiction in terms of meaning.

Now, what I've been doing in this book does not in itself prove anything, of course. But it does reflect the fact that for a very long time human beings have been looking to fiction for meaning. The Homeric poems, the *Iliad* and the *Odyssey*, are often said to mark the beginning of literature in the Western world. In ancient Greek culture these poems were central to the education of the young, not for their beauty and the aesthetic pleasure that beauty could give but for what the student could learn from them—not just about poetry and fiction but about life. And what this seems to indicate is that whether or not the individual work of fiction has a meaning, the human race has for centuries been finding fiction meaningful.

And so we are faced with some questions. How does this sense of the meaningful arise in our experience of fiction? Is there such a thing as *the* meaning of a work of fiction? If some such thing does exist, is it known only after we have finished reading, or is it something that is constantly generated in the process of reading? Is the meaning of a work of fiction fixed forever, or does it change with the passage of time—that is, does "Young Goodman Brown" mean today what it meant when it was first published, well over a century ago? What is the connection between the meaning of the text and the intention of the author?

These questions also, like that of the dividing line between fiction and nonfiction, have troubled critics for some time and probably will continue to do so. Certainly, we shall not in this book settle these matters once and for all. What we may try to do, however, is to arrive at a practical clarification of the issues. And as the word *practical* is meant to convey, our method will be to examine a single fictional text in detail and from a number of angles.

CRITICAL APPROACHES

A number of critical approaches to fiction have evolved over the years, so many that it has been useful to classify them according to their fundamental orientation. M. H. Abrams, in his work *The Mirror and the Lamp*, suggests that the many critical approaches, not just to fiction but to literature in general, fall into four categories. Although Abrams's work has been deservedly influential, it has been suggested that one further heading is required, yielding a total of five. These are as follows:

1. The "mimetic" approach, which is concerned with the relation between the text and the "real world" that the text is supposed to imitate or represent.

2. The "genetic" approach, which is concerned with the relation between the text and its author.

3. The "intertextual" approach, which is concerned with the relation between the text and other texts.

4. The "objective" approach, which is concerned with relationships within the text, or with the text as a system of relationships.

5. The "pragmatic" approach, which is concerned with the relation between the text and the reader.

Now, these approaches are not necessarily mutually exclusive, but what I propose to do is to apply each (or some versions of each) to a single text. For this purpose I choose Hawthorne's "Young Goodman Brown," which you'll find printed as an appendix to this book. The many references already made to this story reflect not only my great admiration for it but also my belief that it is an unusually illustrative example of the strategies of fiction. Now we're going to look at it as the object of critical approaches to fiction. The goal is a clearer response to the question that may be phrased as, how does fiction mean?

THE MIMETIC APPROACH

To begin with the mimetic approach, we've said that this approach is concerned with the relation between the text and the "real world." The text is presumed to be an imitation or representation of the world beyond the text, essentially the world that you and I live in.

One thing that may be said about the mimetic approach is that it's been around for a long time. At least by the time of Plato, who died more than three hundred years before the beginning of the Christian era, the idea of the literary work as imitation or representation (that's the term we'll prefer from this point) was clearly well established, since Plato discusses it in terms that suggest his audience is entirely familiar with the concept. And the mimetic approach remains a popular one, not only among professional and academic critics but, it seems, among readers in general. How many readers read James Michener to learn something about Hawaii, John Jakes to learn something about the Civil War, and lots of other best sellers to learn something about how famous people live? Although, we presume, these readers know that what they are reading is fiction, they also seem to feel that fiction can reliably represent the real world, present or past.

Or consider, at what most critics would claim is a higher or more sophisticated level, a novel like Ann Beattie's *Falling in Place*, which we talked about in our discussion of setting. In that discussion, as you will remember, we noted that the novel's setting is Connecticut's suburbia.

Obviously, one question a mimetic-minded reader might ask is whether Beattie portrays Connecticut's suburbs as they really are. The question would involve measuring the details of the novel against certain realities that exist outside the novel and asking whether they match in some acceptable way.

But as we also said before, there seems to be a larger implication in Beattie's treatment of her setting. That the suburbs in her novel are in all important respects indistinguishable from other suburbs may suggest that one American suburb is very like another and that this is symptomatic of a deeper homogenization of American culture. If this is so, the novel is, by implication, saying something about contemporary American life, both about the surfaces of life and about what those surfaces may mean. Again, it's a matter of measuring what's in the novel against certain realities that exist outside the novel, but the act of measuring has become more complicated.

All of our illustrations so far have assumed a close relationship between representation and realism. Beattie's novel is about America in our time; John Jakes writes of an earlier era, but Jakes's fans presumably trust that what he offers constitutes a realistic reconstruction of the Civil War era. Does this mean that the mimetic approach is appropriate only when we're dealing with realistic fiction?

In fact, in its origins the mimetic approach was not concerned with realism in our sense of the word at all. What literature represents, according to this more traditional view, is not the particulars of a specific time and place—say, suburban America in the last quarter of the twentieth century—but more general or even universal truths about the human condition. This doesn't mean at all that what Ann Beattie writes is not literature, but it may suggest that the literary value of her work doesn't rest ultimately on whether her picture of contemporary American culture is accurate.

Certainly, no one will ever advance "Young Goodman Brown" as a masterpiece of literary realism: witches flying through the air, sticks that turn into snakes, a gathering of the living and the dead, conversations with the devil—all hardly the stuff of realism. Yet, as we'll see, the story can prove responsive to the mimetic approach and can be seen as offering a representation of life.

To begin with, we might give a bit of attention to those features of the text that, without making it realistic, make it most like realism. There are, first of all, those references to actual places, to actual historical figures and events. These may at least have the effect of giving the more fantastic elements of the text a historical-realist point' of departure. And perhaps of greater significance, there is the suggestion that the most fantastic events in the story, including those enumerated above, were in fact all a dream. A suggestion, indeed a question, is all we're talking about, but it may be enough to avoid a collision between what the story deals with and the reader's sense of the real.

But none of this really gets to the heart of the matter. Most of us, I think, would recognize that while the details mentioned above might make it easier for the literal-minded reader to accept the story's fantastic elements, it's still precisely those fantastic elements that remain dominant in the story. And we remain faced with the question of how this kind of fantasy can represent any kind of reality.

Perhaps the phrase "kind of reality" begins to indicate the direction we might take. If we can accept that there is more than one kind of reality, then perhaps we'll be prepared to see Hawthorne's story as a representation of one kind.

Now let's recapitulate the central action of the story. A young man, leaving his wife at home, goes into the forest to keep an appointment with the devil. He has some second thoughts and hesitations, indeed engages in arguments with the devil, who finally leaves him alone in the forest. Yet the young man does arrive at the appointed place for some kind of demonic ceremony—in fact, as we realize, an initiation ceremony. In attendance is a vast crowd that seems to include the entire community and all of those people the young man has been taught to respect, not excepting members of his own family. It turns out that the young man and his wife are both to be initiated on this night into the devil's community, but at the last moment the young man resists the devil and urges his wife to do the same. The next morning the young man awakens in the forest. From that time he is a changed man, withdrawn from the community and even from the bosom of his wife. Living in this state of misery for many years, he finally dies in gloom.

I have, of course, omitted a few things in this account, including all of the historical allusions we've mentioned and the speculation by the narrator that the whole night in the forest and all that it involved may have been a dream. That is, I've deliberately left out those details that bring the story closest to realism, as well as situating the action in a particular time and place. What is left, then, may fairly represent what we've called the fantastic elements.

Now, it's obvious that what we're left with doesn't have the reality of suburbs in Connecticut—doesn't have, that is, the kind of physical, social reality we find in Ann Beattie's novel. But that doesn't mean that no kind of reality is represented in Hawthorne's story. And we might find it useful to explore the possibility that at least one kind of reality represented in "Young Goodman Brown" is psychological reality.

I have in mind the psychology of temptation. Brown has set his mind on doing something that by his own standards he shouldn't do. Let that something be represented by the ceremony in the forest, joining the devil's party. On his way he hesitates and argues with the devil, as you or I, on our way to committing a sin (and to avoid theological dispute, let that mean here some act that violates our deepest sense of who and what we are and ought to be), might hesitate and might argue *with that in ourselves* that seems to be urging us on. So Brown hesitates and argues, but even though the devil abandons the argument, Brown winds up precisely where he intended to go. Perhaps by the time one starts arguing with the devil, with temptation, the argument is already lost.

What Hawthorne offers, in this view, is a kind of insight into psychological reality, insight being in this case the goal of representation. And departures from physical and social reality might be accounted for on grounds that these departures bring the story's psychological concerns more clearly into relief.

But of course, what we've said so far is only part of the story. For Brown is not alone in the forest. And although his instinct—a guilty one—is to conceal himself from Goody Cloyse and from the minister and deacon when they pass by, he finally stands revealed before the whole community, as they are revealed to him. And he stands revealed before his wife, as she is revealed to him. But the devil holds out the promise—or the threat—that still further revelation is to follow:

> By the sympathy of your human hearts for sin ye shall scent out all the places—whether in church, bedchamber, street, field, or forest—where crime has been committed, and shall exult to behold the whole earth one stain of guilt, one mighty blood spot. Far more than this. It shall be yours to penetrate, in every bosom, the deep mystery of sin, the fountain of all wicked arts, and which inexhaustibly supplies more evil impulses than human power—than my power at its utmost—can make manifest in deeds. And now, my children, look upon each other.

And it is as Brown and his wife Faith stand on the verge—"What polluted wretches would the next glance show them to each other, shuddering alike at what they disclosed and what they saw!"—that Brown cries, "look up to heaven and resist the wicked one."

The story of temptation, then, leads to resistance—on Brown's part, apparently successful resistance—to temptation. But the story doesn't end there. Why, we must ask, does Brown's success in resisting temptation lead to his end in gloom? Or at least, what is the connection between the resistance and the gloom?

We note at once that the attention to psychological if not physical reality that characterized earlier passages in the story is not so clearly present here. That is, I understand the psychology of Brown's temptation, and as I've indicated, it rings true. I'm not sure I understand the psychology of his resistance to temptation. Hawthorne doesn't make clear what hitherto hidden resources Brown calls upon at his moment of resistance. In fact, it seems that the story's main focus has shifted from the psychological to the moral.

What Brown might have learned from his night in the forest is that we are all members of the same community—let's call it the community of sinners. What happens instead is that Brown, in resisting, denies his membership in that community, but as we move to the denouement, that denial seems to cut him off from the human community as such.

The devil, we've often been told, is the father of lies. The devil in this story might better be described as the father of half-truths. He calls Brown's attention to the evil that is in all of us, but he is false in his implication that that's the whole truth about us. Brown is unable to accept the true insight into moral (that is, human) complexity that he might have derived from his experience. He continues to think in either-or terms. For Brown, the truth about Goody Cloyse is only the truth of the night in the forest. The daylight Goody Cloyse of the village is, for him, a lie. Seeing all but himself, the one who resisted, as irredeemably evil, he withdraws into himself and dies in gloom.

In "Young Goodman Brown," then, Hawthorne is examining the psychology of temptation, but he is finally offering an insight into the irreducible complexity of the human being. Brown's inability to accept this insight is what explains his apparently dismal fate. And in thus summarizing what seems to me to be implicit in the story as a whole, what the story seems to tell me about the human condition, I am articulating its theme.

In using words like "insight" I imply that what Hawthorne tells me is true—that this work of fiction, even of fantasy, offers a true insight into reality, and that is its meaning.

Now, you might argue that the insight of which we've just been speaking is not a true one, that Hawthorne is wrong about reality in some important way. And you might offer cogent arguments for your position. But you would still be acting as a mimetic critic, still measuring the text against some reality that exists outside the text, and still asking, do they match?

In a famous passage Aristotle, one of the great mimeticists, declares that literature is a higher and more philosophical thing than history; for, while history is limited to the particular, literature can give us the general in and through the particular. Thus, the story of a night spent by a perhaps rather shallow young man in and around Salem village three hundred years ago is also a meditation on some of the deepest and most permanent mysteries of being human. And it's not that part of the story is one thing and part the other; rather, the general and particular are inextricably joined, as occurs in the finest instances of fiction viewed in the perspective of the mimetic approach.

The claim of the mimetic approach, then, is that the meaning of fiction is essentially the insight that it offers us into the real world. In the most traditional and sophisticated version of the mimetic approach, the reality with which fiction is concerned is not limited to the physical, social, and historical but extends as well to the psychological, the moral, and the spiritual.

THE GENETIC APPROACH

But if this is what fiction is about, where does fiction come from? In the preceding discussion, every once in a while I referred to "Hawthorne" or to "the author," reminding us that although I may choose to concentrate on the relationship between the text and the real world at large, fiction—at least in the forms in which we modern readers know it best—originates in an author. And the approach that concerns itself directly with the relationship between text and author we're calling "genetic," since it is concerned with the genesis of the work of fiction.

One form of genetic criticism focuses on the question of the author's intention. In this view, a work of fiction has a meaning because its author intends a meaning, and the intention of the author is the meaning of the work. The job of the reader or critic is essentially to discern and, in writing or speaking about the work, to state the intention of the author.

Note that the mimetic critic and the genetic critic can see eye-to-eye on a number of points in dealing with a particular text. Take what I said before about "Young Goodman Brown." All of that was, I said, from a mimetic perspective. Shifting to a genetic perspective, I might not have to change a thing. The meaning of the story might be in all important respects just as I have stated it. But speaking as a mimetic critic, I don't concern myself with the author's intention. Here, I say, is the text, and here is the world, and here is what they have to do with each other. And ultimately I value the text insofar as I find that it offers true insights into reality.

Speaking, on the other hand, as a genetic critic, I want to know if the author intended the meaning I believe I have found in the text. If the author did not intend it, then no matter how interesting it may be on other grounds, it is simply not the meaning of the text.

But how can I establish that what I take to be the meaning of the text was in fact intended by the author? Concentrating on the text itself, I may argue from a knowledge of literary strategies and conventions, some of the kinds of things we've been discussing in this book. Knowledge of such matters is what we call critical competence, and I'd argue that such knowledge may be presumed to be shared by writer and reader. In the absence of evidence to the contrary, I can assume that Hawthorne writes within a tradition that he and I share. Discerning the writer's intention, then, is not some kind of mind reading act. It's a matter of attending to the particular writer's individual way of realizing the traditional possibilities of fiction.

But it's also true that "tradition" is a big word, and fiction doesn't stand still. Hawthorne wrote "Young Goodman Brown" in the first half of the nineteenth century; we read it in the second half of the twentieth. Is the tradition as we receive it in all important respects as it was for him? We must, that is, be on our guard against anachronistic readings. Is the psychology that I spoke of before a psychology that would have been available to Hawthorne, writing when he did?

In fact, there's nothing so up-to-date, certainly nothing revolutionary (or even very deep) about the psychology I brought to bear on the story, and I've no reason to doubt its availability to Hawthorne. It would be a more complicated question had I tried to apply to the story some of the notions of a later psychological theory like the Freudian; then the question of anachronism might well arise. But of that, more— just a little more—later.

It might be that I'm not satisfied with the sort of general (shared tradition) and negative (no reason to doubt) statements I've been making, and I want stronger, more specific, more positive evidence of Hawthorne's intention in this particular story. Then I may well decide that I must place this story in the context of other texts by Hawthorne to get a sense of how Hawthorne's mind and imagination characteristically work. I need not limit myself in this search to published works of fiction. Unfinished works, works of nonfiction, letters, and journals—all may help me to learn what I want to know. I might even decide as I proceed that I'm more interested in entering the mind of Hawthorne than I am in merely settling the meaning of a single story. In that case, I'm on my way to becoming the sort of genetic critic we call a critic of consciousness.

But I resist that temptation and return to "Young Goodman Brown." And I declare, after having considered all of this evidence, that I was right in the first place. All of the contextual evidence supports my original interpretation, but I am now prepared to introduce passages from "The Birthmark," say, and from "My Kinsman, Major Molineux" in support of my interpretation of "Young Goodman Brown," demonstrating thereby that my reading of "Brown" is consistent with what all the evidence shows to be the characteristic working of the mind and imagination of Nathaniel Hawthorne.

So far, I'm afraid, it may look as though the difference between the mimetic critic and genetic critic is simply that being a genetic critic is a little more complicated—there's an additional question to take into account—and a lot slower. It is, of course, possible (though I don't believe it's the case here) that all of these investigations would bring up some reason to reject our original, mimetically oriented reading. Perhaps a more likely occurrence would be that we might be moved to refine that reading in some way, perhaps to give more attention to Faith as one of "Hawthorne's women." We'd compare and contrast her to figures like Gloriana ("The Birthmark"), Beatrice ("Rappaccini's Daughter"), and Hester Prynne (*The Scarlet Letter*). This might lead not necessarily to a radically new interpretation but to some shadings and subtle shifts of emphasis in the one we've already articulated.

But we haven't yet mentioned the most significant difference between the mimetic and genetic approaches. You remember what we called the story's theme. For the mimetic critic, the ultimate question is whether the theme is true or not, whether the story offers us a true insight into human experience; whereas for the genetic critic as such, the question of truth, of correspondence to some kind of independent reality, simply doesn't arise.

In fact, the word *theme* may be inappropriate in this context. What the genetic critic is primarily interested in isn't so much the theme of the story as the vision of the writer.

The vision of the writer simply means the writer's characteristic way of seeing things. In a way, as a genetic critic I read a Hawthorne story not to learn about the world but to learn about Hawthorne. Or perhaps to learn about Hawthorne's world.

What I mean is this: I see the world from inside my head, and you see the world from inside yours. The power of fiction is that it takes us inside somebody else's head, inside the mind and imagination of the author. When I am reading "Young Goodman Brown," my thoughts are, in a sense, not mine but Hawthorne's. He brings me into the forest, and it's into his forest that he brings me.

And the value of this is that it's finally liberating. The opportunity to enter into this special relationship with Hawthorne and with the other authors I read makes me aware of possible ways of seeing I might never have discovered for myself. According to Shelley, a great geneticist, the imagination is the great agent of moral good. Reading fiction, reading Hawthorne, extends my imagination.

Almost all we've said so far about the genetic approach has been concerned with the author's intention, although intention may seem too cool a word as we begin to raise the question of the author's vision. And we may indeed note that there are two tendencies within genetic criticism. One, the intentionalist tendency, has been the principal subject of our remarks so far. The other, the expressive tendency, begins to emerge in our comments on the author's vision.

The intentionalist tendency emphasizes conscious control; there are, in the strict sense, no unconscious intentions. That's why it may make sense to say that an author intends a specific effect, even that the author intends the meaning of the story, but it seems rather strange to say that Hawthorne intends his vision. It does not, on the other hand, seem nearly so strange to say that the body of an author's work *expresses* his vision, as we might say in Hawthorne's case.

The reason for this difference seems to be that when we speak of a writer's vision we are naming something that we understand as being a mix of the conscious and unconscious. Hawthorne, for example, does not decide on his vision or choose it from a list of possibilities. It seems more accurate, though admittedly metaphorical, to speak of a writer's vision as growing in the writer, arising out of the writer's total—conscious and unconscious—response to the environment.

The notion of expression, then, unlike that of intention, allows for an unconscious component in the creative process. And that brings us back to the Freudians and, for that matter, to all of the twentieth-century explorers of the unconscious. We said before that, in the context of intentionalism, to read "Young Goodman Brown" in the light of Freudian psychology would be anachronistic and therefore unacceptable. As our emphasis shifts to the expressive, the situation changes. If Freud, or the Freudians, or anyone else can provide us with insights into the unconscious components of the creative process, and therefore of the author's vision, we are free to make use of those insights.

Thus, with regard to "Young Goodman Brown," we might be inclined to give closer attention to some details that have hitherto escaped our attention. What, for example, are we to make of the fact that of the great crowd gathered in the forest the only one who seems by gesture to encourage Brown to resist is a woman who may be his mother? That in resisting, Brown turns away not only from the devil but from his wife as well? What symbolism may we discern in the basin, hollowed out of the rock, that contains blood, or liquid flame, or water? Why do Faith's thoughts and dreams make her "afeared of *herself*"? Is there any significance in the fact that in setting forth on his journey, Brown rejects his pretty bride's invitation to join her in bed? Does Brown's status as a recently married man tell us something? Does the fact that Hawthorne's stories often feature young men who have just been married or are just about to be married tell us anything?

Once again, it's not my intention to argue in favor of a single interpretation. But the expressive orientation often leads to questions about what the author reveals, not merely what he intends, and so might lead to an examination of the possibility that certain psychosexual anxieties are revealed in "Young Goodman Brown" and other tales of Hawthorne.

We must in fairness add that a mimetically oriented critic with a Freudian tilt might prefer to say that these tales *represent* sexual anxieties, rather than revealing them, in the sense in which we just used that term.

Genetic criticism, then, locates the meaning of fiction in the relationship between the story and its author. Genetic-intentional criticism sees meaning as the reflection in the text of the author's intention. Genetic-expressive criticism sees it as the expression of the author's vision. Genetic-intentional criticism concerns itself with the conscious; genetic-expressive criticism is open as well to the unconscious. Both give us further grounds for regarding fiction as meaningful.

THE INTERTEXTUAL APPROACH

We noted that one strategy that might be followed by the intentionalist critic is to turn to texts other than the one immediately under consideration. If I want to understand "Young Goodman Brown," it may be advisable for me to read *The Scarlet Letter*, "The Maypole of Merrymount," Hawthorne's journals, and the letters he wrote to his fiancee (later his wife), Sophia Peabody. This remains genetic criticism as long as my purpose continues to be to find out what the author intends or expresses in his or her work. But the activity of placing one text in the context of other texts need not be limited to texts by the same author and need not have as its purpose an examination of the text-author relationship.

That is, it's possible to approach "Young Goodman Brown" by way of other texts, without the genetic bias we've been discussing. It's possible, in other words, to take the intertextual approach.

The basic notion of the intertextual approach, as we're using the term, is that meaning is a matter of language, arising out of the interaction of texts. With the intertextual approach, the question of anachronism dissolves. Although normally there will be some specific reason why I discuss this text in relation to that text, theoretically the reason need be no better than that it occurs to me to do so. If I find that a story by Joyce Carol Oates, Flannery O'Connor, or some other twentieth-century writer casts what I consider an interesting, provocative, or revealing light on the nineteenth-century story "Young Goodman Brown," there is nothing to prevent me from exploring it, although the burden of demonstrating that I have come up with something interesting, provocative, or revealing remains on me.

But I'm being conservative in limiting myself to fiction writers. Any text(s) can be discussed in relation to any other text(s). Ultimately, the context of a text is all texts.

Are you still with me?

The idea of intertextuality is sweeping in its implications, but our purposes don't demand that we examine all of those implications. A more familiar version of intertextuality is the genre study, a study of groups of works that share a sufficient number of significant "family resemblances" to constitute a genre or kind. One of the more familiar genres is the detective story, and we habitually read and think about detective stories in the light of other detective stories, rather than in the light of the insights into reality they offer or what they reveal of the author's vision. On the whole, we prefer the detective story that is enough like other detective stories to satisfy our general expectations and sufficiently different from the others to give us some sense of freshness or surprise. In short, when it comes to detective fiction, almost all of us are intertextualists.

Now, the question for "Young Goodman Brown" is, what other texts do we see it in relation to? One possible answer is in terms of genre. Critics sometimes classify "Young Goodman Brown" as a Gothic tale. This might involve examining "Brown" in relation to works by Horace Walpole, Anne Radcliffe, Monk Lewis, E. T. A. Hoffman, Charles Maturin, Mary Shelley, Charles Brockden Brown, and Edgar Allan Poe; the list is by no means exhaustive. We would not be looking for evidence that Hawthorne was "influenced" by any of these writers, although that might be the concern of a genetic critic exploring precisely the same material. We'd simply be trying to determine where

Hawthorne's story fits in this company. To what extent is his Gothic tale like all other Gothic tales, in what ways is it different, and what is the significance of the differences? The meaning of the text, then, is precisely its relationship to other texts.

But the other texts may be selected on considerations other than those of genre. "Young Goodman Brown" is a story in which the protagonist enters, or considers entering, into some kind of pact with the devil. It is also, as we've seen, a "temptation" story. What other texts come to mind that involve pacts with the devil (e.g., the many versions of the Faust myth)? What about other temptation stories? What light do these cast on the particular treatment of these motifs in "Young Goodman Brown"—for example, on the apparent twist that, for Brown, the evil consequences follow his resisting, not his succumbing to, temptation. What does this suggest about the meaning(s) of temptation and resistance to temptation in "Young Goodman Brown"?

We have only hinted at the possibilities of the intertextual approach. As we've already indicated, there are few theoretical limits to the approach, not surprising in view of the currently fashionable view that all of nature, all of history, all of human experience, and the very personal self (including the self of the author) have been thoroughly "textualized." None of these, it's said, can be seen or known "in themselves" but only by way of an infinity of texts. And so the attempt to relate "Young Goodman Brown" to reality or to the author is hopelessly naive. A text can be related only to other texts.

Well, that's one way of looking at it. And if you look at it that way, you have yet another basis for regarding the work of fiction as meaningful. Fiction means in the same way everything else means, that is, by a process of interaction in a universe of texts.

Intertextuality, then, exists in both a strong and a weak form. The strong form—the only context of a text is all texts—places no theoretical limits on the texts that can be brought into relationship. The weak form requires that texts brought into relationship with one another be demonstrably relevant to one another—for example, belong to the same genre ("Young Goodman Brown" in relation to other Gothic tales) or embody similar motifs (Faustian elements in "Young Goodman Brown" and other texts). And meaning is found in the terms of the relationships thus discovered.

THE OBJECTIVE APPROACH

But it may be objected that in talking of the relationship of "Young Goodman Brown" to so many things beyond the text (reality, the author, and other texts), we risk losing sight of the story in itself. Surely, that's what must remain our principal concern?

And that question brings us to our fourth critical approach, which we're calling the objective. (I'm not especially happy with the term, but the available alternatives are equally unsatisfactory.) The objective approach is so called because, rather than examining the text in its relationships to entities outside the text, it claims to examine the text "in itself," as an independent, self-contained object. Therefore, the relationships with which the objective critic is concerned are relationships within the text, essentially the relationship of part to part and of part to whole.

The objective critic's basic question is, how do these internal relationships, of part to part and part to whole, cohere? How are the parts integrated into the design of the whole?

So in looking at "Young Goodman Brown" from the objective perspective, we look especially for devices that tend to promote coherence. We note, for instance, that the story is organized on the basis of a journey (Brown's journey), following the still more specific pattern of withdrawal and return: Brown withdraws from the village into the forest, then returns to the village. If the terms "journey" and "withdrawal and return" seem to emphasize the spatial, there is temporal organization in the story as well. The main events of the story are not only presented in a roughly chronological order but fall into the pattern sunset-night-sunrise. These patterns, both spatial and temporal, help to organize and give direction to the diverse events of the narrative.

The story also frequently reflects an organization through repetition and variation. Faith's pink ribbons are introduced and emphasized in the opening paragraphs of the story. The emphasis is itself partly a matter of repetition and partly a matter of their irrelevance, at this point, to the plot. That is, since the ribbons don't at this point make anything happen, the reader is inclined to wonder why they are being so ostentatiously mentioned, and that wondering itself lends further emphasis to the ribbons. And all of this points us toward the culminating and climactic repetition, when the sight of Faith's ribbons drives a previously wavering Brown into the heart of the forest.

There are a number of other significant repetitions in "Young Goodman Brown," more indeed than we can examine here. Not all are as explicit as the one we just looked at, focusing as it does on a tangible object like Faith's ribbons. When the minister and deacon pass through the forest, Brown conceals himself, as he has done before when Goody Cloyse appeared. But this repetition of physical concealment is in turn a repetition of the motif of concealment first introduced when Brown conceals his destination and purpose from his wife Faith. And these concealments enter into a relationship of contrast with the initiation scene in the forest, where not concealment but revelation becomes the dominant element. And following this pattern to this point may lead to the perception that Brown's resistance to the devil is yet another act of concealment. Remember that at the moment Brown cries out, he and Faith are about to be exposed to each other and to the entire community. In resisting the devil, Brown also keeps his secrets.

Bringing together what we have already said leads us to see yet another organizing principle at work here, the principle of development. We spoke of repetition and variation. The variation in the "pink ribbons" motif doesn't arise from changes in the object—the ribbons remain the ribbons—but from changes in the context. The ribbons turn up at different stages in the development of the narrative, of the journey, and of the pattern of withdrawal and return. The term *development* suggests that the diverse episodes of the narrative clearly form a larger whole, that we may clearly see the parts in relation to one another and to the whole.

As we move toward the denouement of the story, we move also toward an increasing sense of the interrelationships among the elements that make up the whole story. We begin to see how everything fits and *that* everything fits. At no cost to the liveliness of the story or the interest of the individual episodes, a coherent whole has been formed. In this whole, we can now see, every element has performed its function, made its contribution.

One of the elements contributing to the satisfying closure that the story finally reaches has been its theme. We talked about the theme of the story in the context of the mimetic approach, and the statement of theme we offered there need not be changed in this new context. What does change is the place of the theme in the overall design.

For the mimetic critic, you recall, theme is an articulation of the insight the work offers into the human condition. Theme is the general significance that arises out of and through the particular details of character, situation, and so on that make up the whole story. The strong claim of the mimetic critic is that through the embodiment of theme the work of fiction gives us real knowledge in the form of insight into reality.

In the perspective of the objective approach, theme has quite a different role to play. First, theme—like plot, character, and style—is yet another element to be integrated into the whole. Seen in this light, theme contributes to the complexity of the work, a positive feature as long as it does not prevent the achievement of coherence. But among the elements of fiction, theme makes a special contribution to coherence because it is in the light, finally, of theme that all the other elements fall into place. The theme of "Young Goodman Brown" is what brings it all together.

According to the objective critic, "Young Goodman Brown" may or may not provide us with a true insight into the human condition, but that's not really the issue. What matters is that the theme lends power, complexity, and coherence to the aesthetic object that is the story.

But if the story is to be seen as a self-contained aesthetic object, closing in upon itself, what has become of the idea of meaning? There are several answers to this question.

First, the objective approach has its strong version and its weak version. In its weak version, the objective approach comfortably coexists with other approaches, especially with the mimetic. Here's how it works. The fusion of particular and general in the fictional text celebrated by mimetic critics is dependent on the achievement of form. Form is what distinguishes fiction from life and what permits fiction to present the general truth in the particular. But, the mimetic approach as such has little to say about form; its concern is with what is achieved *through* form. Therefore, the mimetic approach, though sound in itself, must be supplemented. The objective approach, which concentrates on the formal aspect of fiction, is just that supplement.

The strong version of the objective approach makes more sweeping claims. This version rejects the mimetic, along with the genetic and intertextual (as well as the pragmatic, but we haven't come to that yet), as distortions. Its no-compromise position is that the work of fiction is a self-contained aesthetic object and nothing else.

Yet even here, the notion of meaning lives. The story as aesthetic object doesn't *mean*, in quite the sense we've been using that word, but it contains meaning. This has a number of implications, but we'll develop just one of them. A story's theme is a meaningful, if implicit, statement about the human condition. The strong objective critic doesn't deny that a story has a theme but merely insists that the theme be seen in relation to the rest of the story, rather than in relation to the world outside the story. That is, the theme cannot be isolated from the concrete particulars that make up the rest of the story.

And this, it might be argued, is the true wisdom of fiction. Fiction does not give us separable meanings that can be applied at large to any and all situations. Rather, fiction gives us the play of meaning and matter. The theme of "Young Goodman Brown" is "true" for the story. That is, it relates vitally to everything in the story. In that, it's like all of the authentic meanings of our lives—not generalizations to be used as needed, not the particular as the illustration of meaning, but the particular, here and now, as itself meaningful. Life, let's say, is not something meant but something lived, and it's in the living that we find whatever meaning there is. But whatever meaning we find is always tentative, provisional, and temporary for now. And fiction viewed as object enacts precisely this relationship of meaning to the matter of life.

THE PRAGMATIC APPROACH

But, we may ask, if fiction is viewed as object, who does the viewing? The answer, it seems, must be the reader, and that answer threatens or promises to reopen the closed world of the story as self-contained object.

This is not, in fact, the first appearance the reader has made in these proceedings. In a way, the reader has been the "dirty little secret" of the approaches we've been considering. It is the reader who performs the operation of relating text to world, to author, and to other texts and, as we just noted, for whom the text may be a self-contained aesthetic object. And if you look carefully, you'll find that the reader's presence has been implicitly acknowledged again and again in the course of this chapter.

We have already, in the chapter "Fiction and the Reader," said something about this vital relationship, and we won't repeat here what we said there. We'll summarize it briefly in this way: through the activation of worldly knowledge and critical competence, the reader constructs the meaning of the story. Now we'll look at some other aspects of the pragmatic approach, our name for the critical approach that concerns itself with the relationship between the text and the reader.

Form, we have seen, is a primary concern of the objective critic. But for the objective critic the form of fiction closes in upon itself and can be contemplated only by the reader. A different view of form has been suggested by Kenneth Burke. Form, in Burke's view, is "the psychology of the reader." Elaborating on this, Burke defines form as "the creation of appetites in the reader and the adequate satisfaction of those appetites." The creation and satisfaction are both the work of form. Let's examine how this approach might be applied to "Young Goodman Brown."

We might, first of all, note that we bring some appetites to the story—primarily, we might suppose, an appetite for narrative. That is, we want to be told a story. And even if we've never worked it out systematically, we have some idea of what a story is. To what extent the appetite for narrative is inborn and to what extent learned need not concern us here. The more recent tendency in theoretical discussions of the point has been to emphasize the learned—that is, the culturally determined—over claims for the inborn or natural.

The appetites created by the particular story, then, work within the framework of our prior appetite for narrative. If the story deviates too much from our prior notions of what narrative is, of what a story is, we'll have difficulty in processing the text, in constructing the story's meaning and recognizing its coherence. What our "prior notions" are depends in large part on our previous experience with fiction. A consequence of that is that a story that seems difficult to one reader may not seem so difficult to another.

"Young Goodman Brown" is a demanding story but not one that deviates radically from what we may suppose to be a reasonably experienced reader's understanding of what a story is. It is not difficult in that sense.

The scenic opening of the story isn't exactly "Once upon a time," but most readers can process it with little difficulty. References like the one to Salem village call on the reader's wordly knowledge, as do such things as the meaning of "wife" and the nature of the institution of marriage within which that word has its meaning. Most of us have that kind of knowledge in adequate supply.

We very quickly recognize the presence of conflict, and that recognition brings into play the creation of appetites by the story itself. Brown is on the verge of leaving; his wife wants him to stay. Where do we stand? I'm suggesting that we may be more involved than we recognize.

Since we've just met the characters, let's say that we are not likely at this point to take sides between them. Nor have we any stake in their relationship as such. But perhaps what we see here is a tension between two desires, both of which are known to us, both of which we may well find sympathetic.

Let's call the first of these the desire for comfort and solace. It's the desire that tells us to stay in bed in the morning. It's the desire that here would unite Brown and Faith in the marital bed. It's an understandable desire, but it doesn't promise much of a story, if only because in this context it's so easily realized. If Brown goes back to bed with Faith, that's it. A situation in which the desire for comfort and solace can be realized only after great difficulties have been overcome would hold out a very different kind of narrative promise.

The other desire we can call the desire for adventure. Now, as this story is set up, the second desire is the one that looks more promising. Once Brown crosses the threshold and strides away from his home, the situation is open and alive with possibilities.

And what does this mean? It means that for reasons that have nothing to do with morality, say, and everything to do with our desire for a story, we're on Brown's side. We want him to make that journey before we have any idea where it's going to lead.

That there is some doubt at first as to where Brown is headed only intensifies our desire, for that arouses our curiosity, and our desire that our curiosity be satisfied is in this case synonymous with a desire that Brown move toward his destination.

We are now in a better position to see what's going on in what, in an earlier chapter, we called the "debate" between Brown and the devil. On the one hand, as we mentioned in our discussion of dialogue, we're being provided with information. But that's not what I want to emphasize here. It is perhaps more important that the debate contributes to creating and sustaining appetites in the reader (that's you and me).

Our worldly knowledge is very much involved here, especially what we think we know about how people should behave. They should, as we've so often been told, renounce the devil and his works and resist his snares and temptations. What Brown should now do is, we might suppose, perfectly clear.

But again, if he does it, the story's over. And what kind of a story would that be: a young man sets out on a perilous journey but then changes his mind and goes back home. No, our sense of narrative, our "narrative appetite," demands that Brown, having started on his journey, must complete it. The debate, insofar as it creates, however faintly, some anxiety that he might not complete the journey, only makes us more eager to see that he does.

Let's face it: we're on the devil's side. We *don't want* Brown to turn back. And this is true even though we know, and strongly know, that he should turn back. We said when applying the mimetic approach to this story that it represents the psychology of temptation. What we're saying now is that it's Hawthorne's powerful achievement to force the reader to act out temptation. That is, I the reader must here recognize a conflict between what I think is right and what I want. Hawthorne has put me in a position not so very different from that of Brown himself.

And this is only the beginning. We cannot here carry this reading all the way through the text, although I certainly invite the reader to do so. What we can do is recognize the interaction of text and reader as an essential component of fiction.

I have, by the way, been supposing a fairly cooperative reader of Hawthorne's story, one who is prepared to respond pretty much as Hawthorne wants him to. But the pragmatic approach requires us to recognize the possibility of reading against the grain, that is, of approaching the text from one's own idiosyncratic or ideological angle and refusing to perform docilely the operations the text seems to expect of one. Feminist critics, for instance, have in our time given a good deal of attention to Hawthorne in general and to this story in particular. Some see Hawthorne as almost a sort of protofeminist, emphasizing the power with which Hawthorne situates Faith in a context in which her identity is defined by a patriarchal society. So if she has thoughts and dreams that are at odds with what Puritan society says women should think and dream about, this makes her "afeared of herself" rather than critical of the society whose definitions have apparently failed to take her, her thoughts, and her dreams into account. Others have found evidence of sexism in Hawthorne himself, and for still others it is Hawthorne's confusions and uncertainties about women and their place in society, not his feminism or sexism, that must be faced and understood. The point is that none of these critics is much concerned with whether this is the "right" way to read the story, the way that best responds to the design of the story as we have it. Rather, their claim is that these issues are now on our minds, and it is always appropriate to read in the light of things we care about.

One further emphasis that is especially, if not exclusively, associated with the pragmatic approach is the emphasis on the temporality of the reading process. We read in time—one word, one phrase, one sentence, one paragraph after another. The reading process is just that—a process. And the pragmatic critic would argue that if fiction is meaningful, that means reading fiction is meaningful. But a meaningful process is not the same as a meaningful product. The meaning is not something we arrive at when the story is over but something we are producing at every stage of the process.

Let's be specific. In our discussion of "Young Goodman Brown," we were taking the position that the devil is to be renounced and that temptation is to be resisted. That's what makes our narrative appetite—that Brown should continue on his journey—a bit troubling. But, later in the story Brown *does* resist temptation and renounce the devil. And the last word on Brown is "gloom." It turns out, then, that resisting temptation and renouncing the devil are not unambiguously good.

Does this mean that we were wrong to read the earlier passages as we did? Not at all. In the process of reading this story, we might say we move from one notion of temptation to another, and that movement is part of the meaning. In this view, meaning itself is process—not fixed but constantly in flux. And the reading process is meaningful in part because it captures that quality of meaning.

CONCLUSION: It should be clear that except in the case of the more extreme forms of what we've called the strong versions of some of these approaches, it is not necessary to choose among them. The pragmatic approach, for instance, does not contradict, say, the mimetic approach so much as it raises a different set of questions about the text. I'll remove the mask long enough to say that I personally believe everything I've said throughout this book about "Young Goodman Brown." I guess that makes me a champion of the mimetic-genetic-intertextual-objective-pragmatic approach. And that sounds about right to me.

CHAPTER EIGHT
EVALUATION

INTRODUCTION: There is a sense in which this chapter is not justified. What I mean is, a separate chapter on evaluation is at least questionable because evaluation isn't a separate act, something that occurs after the reading is over. Rather, evaluation is an integral part of the reading process; that's why evaluation has already come up so many times in the course of this book. In talking about character, for example, we rejected the standard of lifelikeness in favor of relevance; we were talking about a criterion for evaluating the author's presentation of character. We have often talked of the importance of placing any single element in a story in the context of the story as a whole. There's a criterion implicit in that; a successful work of fiction is not merely a collection of isolated moments but some kind of integrated or coherent whole.

In short, we've been discussing evaluation all along. And all we mean to do in this chapter is to look back at what we've already said, and in the process perhaps make it all more explicit and a bit more systematic.

AUTHORITY OF CRITICAL CRITERIA: Before we say anything more about critical criteria, let's face the question of what authority such criteria can claim. Can anyone really say what makes a story good or bad, successful or unsuccessful?

Well, not really. That is, just as there are no final judgments on stories and their authors (literary reputations often fluctuate), neither are there criteria of judgment that may be regarded as beyond revision. In fact, even in my lifetime (not so long as all that) I've seen criteria like "sincerity" and "simplicity" pretty much disappear from serious criticism. Taking the longer view, the criterion of originality, in our sense of the word, didn't really gain acceptance until the end of the eighteenth century or the beginning of the nineteenth. Criteria, then, come and go.

And since criteria come and go, we may ask, how can we base judgments on them? There are several answers to this question. One is that criteria come and go but rather slowly. At any given time, there's likely to be something approaching consensus on the question of what constitute appropriate criteria. In fact, differences in terminology may obscure how close we are to consensus on some issues. If one critic praises the coherence of the work; another, its unity; and a third, its integrity, it may well be the case that they are all talking about the same thing. It is also sometimes the case that critics allow their criteria to remain implicit and thereby risk giving the impression that there is greater diversity on these matters than is the case.

Moreover, we may question whether it's accurate to say that we base judgments on criteria. It may be that criteria are merely classifications, ways of imposing some order on the judgments we are making anyway. Do judgments follow criteria, or is it the other way around?

I am sometimes moved to question whether there are any literary criteria for determining whether we are dealing with good literature, as distinguished from literary categories for determining whether we are dealing with literature at all. (Not that I'm absolutely confident that such categories exist, but that's another story.) Perhaps the only criteria are broadly human criteria, since, as we've indicated before, the work of fiction is a human act, the product of human work. Thus, a work of fiction is to be praised if it is wise or honest or compassionate, say, and dispraised to the extent that it fails to measure up to criteria like these. Certainly, it would seem very strange to hear a story being praised for being foolish or dishonest.

Many critics, however, would question the propriety of allowing literary judgment to be thus absorbed into the realm of what they might see as too generally moral criteria. They would insist, I believe, that while these criteria may properly contribute to the final judgment, they are not adequate in themselves.

Another approach, one that focuses more precisely on fiction, seems called for. A criterion that may do the job is: a story is good insofar as it does particularly well the sort of thing that stories do. Now, the sort of thing that stories do has been the subject of this book. Stories organize materials drawn from human experience into plots involving characters, setting, and so on. On the basis of what we were talking about in the previous chapter, we might make that "meaningfully organize." If we try to turn this into a relatively systematic list of criteria, it would, I suggest, include the following items:

COHERENCE: This develops the term *organize*. As we noted in talking about "Young Goodman Brown," one of the things that makes Hawthorne's story so satisfying is our gradually coming to perceive how everything fits and *that* everything fits. Human experience, the stuff that is the ultimate source of fiction, is notoriously unorganized; to organize it into a coherent work of fiction is therefore an accomplishment to be respected.

COMPLEXITY: A story that is merely coherent offers no more than a kind of mechanical satisfaction. Coherence is most admirable when it is most difficult to achieve. A story is complex insofar as the elements it involves are many or varied. It is also complex insofar as the individual elements are allowed to take on a life of their own, as well as contributing to the whole. Look again at the debate between Brown and the devil in "Young Goodman Brown." It's essential to the design of the whole and fulfills its function in that regard with a fine economy, yet it has its own qualities, among them humor and suspense; it's not just a cog in the narrative machinery.

HUMANITY: A story *is* a human act that *does* have its origins in human experience, and that seems to make this an appropriate criterion. We don't mean to suggest by this criterion that stories should be nice. They may, like "Young Goodman Brown," be quite disturbing in their implications. The point is, a good story *has* implications and *is* about the human condition. This, of course, is a development of the term *meaningfully* in our earlier formulation. The meaning has to be meaning for us, and we're human. At this point, by the way, we may reintroduce, as aspects of humanity, such criteria as wisdom, honesty, and compassion.

COMMAND: The author's mastery of the craft of fiction. The ability, for instance, to engage the reader and to sustain and intensify that engagement as the story develops. Look again at our discussion of "Young Goodman Brown" from a pragmatic perspective for an appreciation of Hawthorne's command.

A quality like command can carry us a long way toward finding in favor of a story, and this suggests that what I've just offered shouldn't be treated as a checklist against which a story is to be measured point-by-point. A story that meets in some striking way any of the criteria is likely to please us mightily, even if it should fall a bit short on one or more of the others.

Again, these criteria are not offered as the last word on the subject. But I'll say this on their behalf. Although I arrived at them by the steps outlined earlier in this chapter, they turn out *not* to be highly original. I regard that as good thing because it suggests consensus.

It also seems desirable to have some criteria in mind as a way of enabling conversation about fiction. If we agree that coherence is desirable but disagree on our evaluation of a particular story, we may be able to discuss our disagreement to our mutual benefit and in the process come to a deeper understanding of both the story in question and fiction in general. If, on the other hand, we have no shared notion of the quality we think a story ought to have, the situation is far less promising.

The worst kind of evaluation is the kind that leads nowhere. That's why statements like "It's boring" are boring. A properly articulated evaluation should lead back to the text and should promote, as we suggested above, a deeper understanding of the text. Evaluation is ideally not the end of the process. Evaluation leads to understanding.

CHAPTER NINE
TYPES OF FICTION

INTRODUCTION: *Fiction* is an inclusive term, one that covers many forms, but my working assumption in this book has been that for most of us today, fiction means primarily the short story and the novel. And most of what we've been talking about in the course of our discussion applies equally well to either one. Plot, character, setting, and so on are elements of both the novel and the short story.

In this relatively brief chapter, we are going to look at some of the more notable differences between the novel and the short story; our discussion will be intentionally suggestive, rather than exhaustive. We'll also examine some of the relationships between these two forms and some of their near neighbors—fable and tale for the short story, romance for the novel.

But before moving on to those topics, it might be well if one last time we examine an inclusive feature, that is, one that applies more or less equally to novel and short story. We have discussed such matters as plot, character, setting, tone, and theme. Although we have taken up each of these in turn, we've also insisted that they interact to produce the finished story. And we were suggesting before that the intensity of interaction among the elements to produce a whole that is coherent and meaningful is a criterion of excellence.

DOMINANT ELEMENTS: But there are many avenues to coherence and meaning. The elements we've been discussing interact in a fully realized story but not always as equals. Often we recognize that one or another of these elements provides the basic principle of organization in a story; it becomes, in effect, that in relation to which we see everything else in the story. When a single element from among those we've been discussing takes on this central role in a story, we'll call that element the dominant.

Remember, that one element becoming the dominant doesn't mean that the other elements disappear, only that they assume a subordinate position. Now let's consider some of the possibilities.

PLOT: Plot may be the dominant. When this is the case, our main concern as we read is the unfolding of events. Characters cease to claim our interest as representations of human beings and tend toward the purely functional—that is, they become almost exclusively causal agents in the plot, interesting simply for what they do, rather than for what they are. Setting is either neutral or chosen to heighten our interest in the plot (the exotic setting of an adventure story). Style generally aims for efficiency, rather than calling attention to its own beauties or intricacies.

Examples of stories dominated by plot (or "plot stories") would include most detective stories and suspense thrillers in general. The tale, which we'll discuss below, tends to be dominated by plot.

CHARACTER: A second possibility is domination by character, producing what is sometimes called the character study. In the strong version, the story dominated by character focuses on a single character, with all other elements, including all other characters, becoming subordinate to that one. Classic examples of character as dominant include Willa Cather's "Paul's Case," Katherine Anne Porter's "The Jilting of Granny Weatherall," James Thurber's "The Secret Life of Walter Mitty," and Isaac Bashevis Singer's "Gimpel the Fool."

SETTING: Setting may also be the dominant. A good deal of fiction takes as its subject the struggle between a central character and a hostile or stifling environment, sometimes with the result that it's hard to determine which is the dominant. (In such a case, as we've said before, the very difficulty is significant.) But in a story like James Joyce's "Araby," in spite of the undeniable richness of the whole, setting seems to be the dominant.

THEME: And of course theme may be the dominant. That is, characters, events, setting, and all the rest may take on much of their interest because of their relationship to the story's theme and what the story implies about the human conditon. Many of the stories of Nathaniel Hawthorne, including "The Birthmark" and "Young Goodman Brown," are masterpieces of the theme story. And our many comments on "Young Goodman Brown" should suggest that a great theme story is not merely a thin, intellectualized illustration but rather the rich imaginative realization of a theme.

THE "MOOD STORY": One further possibility is the "mood story," a name we'll use for those stories (usually not held in the highest critical esteem) that seem designed to produce a strongly focused emotional response in the reader. Tear-jerkers like Erich Segal's Love Story, horror stories that concentrate on scaring the reader rather than engaging the reader's imagination, and pornographic stories (perhaps the paradigm of the class) are examples.

RECOGNITION OF THE DOMINANT: The value of recognizing the dominant in a work of fiction is that it tends to promote the appropriate and relevant response. If we read one of the better Sherlock Holmes stories (say, "The Speckled Band") in the light of the fixed idea that complexity of characterization is the defining note of good fiction, we're likely to feel we're wasting our time; if we read it, properly, as an example of plot as dominant, we may well be dazzled by Arthur Conan Doyle's command.

A further implication of what we have just said is that the general criteria introduced in the preceding chapter must always be adapted to the particulars of the story at hand. Recognition of the dominant can be a useful step in the direction of that necessary adaptation.

We must repeat, before leaving this topic, that recognition of the dominant does not mean that the other elements of fiction simply go away. There are characters in "The Speckled Band"; "Young Goodman Brown" does have a plot. The question of how the elements interact in the story as a whole is always relevant, even when one of the elements is the dominant.

We should also make clear that not all works of fiction *have* a dominant in our sense. Even in these cases the idea of the dominant can be a useful critical tool; the recognition that no single element dominates may help to sharpen the reader's responses. Finally, such a work may often be made up of episodes and passages, each of which has its own dominant.

Again, most of what we've been saying applies equally well to the short story and novel. Yet the experience of reading a short story differs in many ways from that of reading a novel, and some discussion of the peculiar qualities of the two forms seems in order.

THE SHORT STORY

A short story is short, and a novel is relatively long. More specifically, the term *short story* is normally applied to works of fiction ranging in length from five hundred to fifteen thousand words. Novels, on the other hand, generally contain at least forty-five thousand words and are often very much longer than that: Samuel Richardson's *Clarissa* runs to over one million words. The "average" length of a modern novel is probably between 80,000 and 150,000 words—obviously, not an especially helpful statistic. Works of prose fiction above fifteen thousand and below forty-five thousand words are called by several names, of which "novella" seems the most widely used. Length itself may seem a purely mechanical consideration, but many of the important qualitie that tend to distinguish the short story from the novel are clearly related to length.

The short story, for instance, is not merely a truncated novel, nor is it part of an unwritten or yet to be written novel. It's true that works originally published as short stories sometimes later turn up as chapters in novels, but you'll usually find that extensive revision has taken place along the way. The length of a good short story is an essential part of the experience of the story.

For many, Edgar Allan Poe settled the matter of the short story's length once and for all when he said that a short story should be short enough to be read at a single sitting. Poe also said that the story should be long enough to produce the desired effect on the reader. From Poe's rules we can derive another: the effect sought in a short story should be one that can be achieved in a single sitting.

INTENSITY: And what kind of effect is appropriate to the short story? Ultimately, of course, that question must be answered by the writers of fiction themselves, and it is certainly not our intention here to tell them what to do. On the basis of past experience, though, we may observe that the short story seems particularly suited to effects of intensity and to exploitation of the elements of fiction that tend to such effects.

PLOT AND INTENSITY: The plot of the short story will often turn on a single incident. Let's consider "My Kinsman, Major Molineux" by Hawthorne. The protagonist of this story is "a young man from the provinces," a type that has always fascinated novelists. The young man wants to make his way in the world, and in this desire we certainly have a subject out of which a novel could emerge. In fact, one could scarcely count the number of novels that have been written on just that subject.

But Hawthorne's interests lie elsewhere. He presents us with a single night in the life of Robin, more specifically with Robin's search for his kinsman. But this night is an especially significant one—in fact, a major turning point—in Robin's life. He had arrived in town to seek the protection of his kinsman, but by the end of the story his kinsman is in disgrace and Robin is told, "You may rise in the world without the help of your kinsman, Major Molineux."

The short story is commonly based on a single incident that proves to be of great significance to the characters. Young Goodman Brown's night in the forest or the arrival of two tough guys at a small town diner ("The Killers")—such incidents are typical of the short story.

CHARACTER AND INTENSITY: Development implies time, and the writer of the short story has relatively little time at his disposal. Not surprisingly then, the short story is as likely to be constructed on the basis of revelation as development. With reference to character, for instance, "The Killers" gives us Nick Adams, its protagonist, as he is at one stage in his development. It does not trace his development beyond this stage. "My Kinsman, Major Molineux" brings Robin to a moment of revelation, then leaves him. "Young Goodman Brown" turns on the revelations of the night in the forest.

TIME AND INTENSITY: The two Hawthorne stories and "The Killers" share another element in common: each deals with actions limited to a single evening. (The last paragraphs of "Young Goodman Brown" extend the time element there, but essentially it remains the story of one night in Brown's life.) Not all short stories limit themselves in this way, but the writer of the short story is naturally drawn to such limited time periods.

To summarize, we associate the short story with compression, concentration, and intensity. These qualities are related to the length of the story and to the structural qualities the length suggests.

THE NOVEL

Where the short story compresses, the novel expands. For the intensity of the short story, the novel substitutes such qualities as range, diversity, and variety. These assertions may provide a starting point for our discussion of the novel.

TIME AND THE NOVEL: The novel is decidedly not meant to be read at a single sitting. Because of its length and because in a way we "live with" a novel for a while, the novel is admirably suited, as the short story is not, to deal with such subjects as the effect of the passage of time on character and on relationships among characters. Such works as Tolstoy's *War and Peace* and Thackeray's *Vanity Fair* are especially notable examples of the novel's power in treating this subject.

DEVELOPMENT: One effect of the passage of time is the *development* of character. The novel permits us to watch this development. A favorite subject of novelists is the growth of a character from childhood to maturity. Dickens's *David Copperfield* and Joyce's *Portrait of the Artist as a Young Man* are two classic examples.

In the last chapter, we mentioned coherence and complexity as critical criteria. Is it too much of an oversimplification to suggest that the short story appeals especially to our demand for coherence and the novel to our demand for complexity? Certainly, the novel affords finer opportunities than does the short story for the expansion of episodes, the development of their intrinsic possibilities, on the way to the denouement. The episodic plot we discussed earlier is traditionally more common in the novel than in the short story. And don't we all feel instinctively that an unfinished short story would hold rather little interest, whereas an unfinished novel might be well-worth reading?

THE ROMANCE NOVEL: A near relation of the novel is the romance. The distinction between the two isn't always easy to see, but on the whole, the novel has tended to be more realistic, more oriented toward the contemporary, and more concerned with the complexities of life in society. The romance has been more inclined to idealization (more heroic heroes, more villainous villains, and conflicts involving clashes of absolutes), more oriented to the past or to imaginary times and places, and to settings removed from contemporary society. As I've said, the dividing line is sometimes unclear (again, it's a matter of gradation), but Richard Chase, in a controversial but highly influential book, has argued that the tradition of the American novel might be better understood as a tradition of the romance. His point is that the longer narratives of James Fenimore Cooper, Nathaniel Hawthorne, Herman Melville, and Mark Twain correspond more to our description of romance than of novel.

THE FABLE AND THE TALE: Two near relations of the short story are the fable and the tale. The fable is a short narrative, often involving humanized animals as characters, and designed to point out a moral. The fable is thus a strong example of what we have called the theme story. It differs from the short story dominated by theme in that, unlike the short story, it tends to reduce to a minimum elements other than theme. Insofar as it may permit a more complex interaction among elements, the fable is moving in the direction of the short story, and, once again, a full study of the topic would have to deal with gradations and borderline cases.

The tale, another near relation of the short story, differs from it in several respects. The tale, as we said above, is a form of plot story. Its primary concern is events, often of a wonderful kind, and it's often loosely constructed, covering indefinite periods of time and stressing temporal rather than causal relations. It differs from short stories dominated by plot in that such stories allow for more interaction among the elements, focus more on causal relations, and tend more toward realism. Again, there are gradations and borderline cases. Is Washington Irving's "Adventures of Rip Van Winkle" a short story or a tale?

APPENDIX ONE
STUDY QUESTIONS

What follows may be regarded as an unsystematic outline, in the form of questions, of chapters 1 through 8 of this book. The questions are intended to help to bring your reading of fiction into sharper critical focus. They also may be of use to students trying to find a workable approach to writing critical papers about fiction. Your answer to almost any one of these questions could be the basis of a successful paper.

NARRATIVE STRUCTURE (Chapter One)

1. To what extent does the story present events in chronological order? Where does the story deviate from chronological order? What functions seem to be served by any deviations from chronological order?

2. Can you see the events that constitute the resolution of the story as the final effects in a causal chain?

3. How efficiently does the beginning of the story perform the function of exposition? What information is imparted about character, situation, and setting? What elements of instability are suggested and by what means?

4. What do you regard as the central conflict of the story? What is its climax? Trace the steps by which the story moves from the emergence of conflict to the climax.

5. Is the denouement, or outcome, of the story plausible in the light of all that has gone before?

6. Is the outcome of the story in any way surprising? How is the surprise achieved? Does the surprise make the outcome less plausible or convincing? If not, why not?

7. As the story unfolds, is there anything about which we are in suspense? How is the suspense created and sustained?

8. Is your interest in the story primarily teleological or episodic? That is, are you primarily interested in where the story is headed, in how things are going to come out, or are you more interested in the individual episodes for their own sake? What qualities of the story lead you to answer as you do?

CHARACTER (Chapter Two)

1. Do the characters of the story seem lifelike? If not, do they seem in some other way(s) relevant to human nature as we know it?

2. What contribution is made by each character, or at least by each major character, to the design of the whole story?

3. How would you define the overall relationship of character and plot in the story?

4. Can you find examples of simple and complex characters in the story? What functions are served by each?

5. Do any of the characters develop or change in the course of the story? Are these changes convincing? Why or why not?

6. Are the characters presented in terms of a balance of social, physical, and psychological traits, or does one kind of trait seem to dominate?

7. What methods of characterization does the story employ? Does any one method seem to be preferred?

8. What motivation is provided for the characters' most important actions?

SETTING (Chapter Three)

1. Are the settings in the story absolutely neutral, or do they have some more significant relation to character and plot?

2. Does the setting approach character and plot in importance?

3. Is setting used metaphorically?

4. How does setting contribute to atmosphere?

5. Is character seen as the effect of setting? Does the story focus on conflicts between character and setting? Does setting contribute positively to self-discovery or spiritual renewal in any of the characters?

POINT OF VIEW (Chapter Four)

1. From what point of view is the story told? What seem to be the principal advantages or disadvantages of this point of view in relation to the story as a whole?

2. If third-person limited point of view is employed, define the relation between narrator and viewpoint character. Do they seem to see things and to say things in pretty much the same way, or is there some considerable distance between them?

3. Is the viewpoint character (or the narrator in first-person narration) the protagonist? If not, what role does this character play in the story? What seems to have dictated the author's choice of narrator or viewpoint character?

4. If first-person point of view is employed, does the story give us any reason to doubt the narrator's reliability?

STYLE AND TONE (Chapter Five)

1. In what ways and to what extent does the style in which the story is written seem appropriate to the story as a whole?

2. Does the diction the author employs seem designed to exploit the connotative, suggestive powers of language, or is it more severely restricted to the denotative level?

3. Is the style strikingly concrete or abstract? Do any images take on significance as a result of frequent repetition?

4. Is figurative language an important feature of the style? Do you find any pattern or consistency in the author's use of figures of speech?

5. Does symbolism play an important role in this story?

6. Is the syntax characteristically simple or complex? In what ways are such syntactical features functional or appropriate to the story as a whole?

7. Is the tone characterized by understatement? hyperbole? something in between? Does irony play an important role?

STRUCTURE AND TECHNIQUE (Chapter Six)

1. What principles of selection seem to be at work in passages of description? Do any of these passages suggest nonphysical qualities of persons, places, or things through description of their physical qualities?

2. What relationship is established between the scenic and the panoramic? What functions are served by each?

3. Does dialogue serve to reveal character? Does each major character have his or her distinctive style of dialogue? Does the dialogue tend to confirm what we know about character by other means?

4. In what ways may the dialogue be described as a selection from human speech? What balance of the natural and artificial do you find in the dialogue?

5. What is the relation of the dialogue passages to the style of the nondialogue passages in the story?

MEANING AND VALUE (Chapter Seven)

1. Does the story as a whole seem to imply some insight into human nature or the human condition? Can you articulate the theme of the story?

2. Does placing the story in the context of other stories by the same author cast any light on the story's meaning, or help you to recognize the author's intention?

3. Can you distinguish between meanings the author probably intended and others the story seems to reveal regardless of, and perhaps in spite of, the author's intentions?

4. Does the story belong to a recognizable genre? What is its relation to other examples of the genre?

5. How are the elements of the story brought into a coherent relationship to one another? Are there any details that dont't seem to fit?

6. How does the story work to create and satisfy appetites (for example, curiosity) in you as you read it?

7. Does the story, whatever the author's intention may have been, confirm or contradict your political, social, moral, religious, or cultural views? How does this affect your overall experience of the story?

EVALUATION (Chapter Eight)

1. Does the story meet the criteria of coherence, complexity, humanity, and command? What are the story's principal strengths and weaknesses in the light of these criteria?

2. Can you suggest further relevant criteria for judging fiction?

APPENDIX TWO
YOUNG GOODMAN BROWN

NATHANIEL HAWTHORNE

Young Goodman Brown came forth at sunset into the street at Salem village; but put his head back, after crossing the threshold, to exchange a parting kiss with his young wife. And Faith, as the wife was aptly named, thrust her own pretty head into the street, letting the wind play with the pink ribbons of her cap while she called to Goodman Brown.

"Dearest heart," whispered she, softly and rather sadly, when her lips were close to his ear, "prithee put off your journey until sunrise and sleep in your own bed to-night. A lone woman is troubled with such dreams and such thoughts that she's afeared of herself sometimes. Pray tarry with me this night, dear husband, of all nights in the year."

"My love and my Faith," replied young Goodman Brown, "of all nights in the year, this one night must I tarry away from thee. My journey, as thou callest it, forth and back again, must needs be done 'twixt now and sunrise. What, my sweet, pretty, wife, dost thou doubt me already, and we but three months married?"

"Then God bless you!" said Faith, with the pink ribbons; "and may you find all well when you come back."

"Amen!" cried Goodman Brown. "Say thy prayers, dear Faith, and go to bed at dusk, and no harm will come to thee."

So they parted; and the young man pursued his way until, being about to turn the corner by the meeting-house, he looked back and saw the head of Faith still peeping after him with a melancholy air, in spite of her pink ribbons.

"Poor little Faith!" thought he, for his heart smote him. "What a wretch am I to leave her on such an errand! She talks of dreams, too. Methought as she spoke there was trouble in her face, as if a dream had warned her what work is to be done to-night. But no, no; 't would kill her to think it. Well, she's a blessed angel on earth; and after this one night I'll cling to her skirts and follow her to heaven."

With this excellent resolve for the future, Goodman Brown felt himself justified in making more haste on his present evil purpose. He had taken a dreary road, darkened by all the gloomiest trees of the forest, which barely stood aside to let the narrow path creep through, and closed immediately behind. It was all as lonely as could be; and there is this peculiarity in such a solitude, that the traveller knows not who may be concealed by the innumerable trunks and the thick boughs overhead; so that with lonely footsteps he may yet be passing through an unseen multitude.

"There may be a devilish Indian behind every tree," said Goodman Brown to himself; and he glanced fearfully behind him as he added, "What if the devil himself should be at my very elbow!"

His head being turned back, he passed a crook of the road, and, looking forward again, beheld the figure of a man, in grave and decent attire, seated at the foot of an old tree. He arose at Goodman Brown's approach and walked onward side by side with him.

"You are late, Goodman Brown," said he. "The clock of the Old South was striking as I came through Boston, and that is full fifteen minutes agone."

"Faith kept me back a while," replied the young man, with a tremor in his voice, caused by the sudden appearance of his companion, though not wholly unexpected.

It was now deep dusk in the forest, and deepest in that part of it where these two were journeying. As nearly as could be discerned, the second traveller was about fifty years old, apparently in the same rank of life as Goodman Brown, and bearing a considerable resemblance to him, though perhaps more in expression than features. Still they might have been taken for father and son. And yet, though the elder person was as simply clad as the younger, and as simple in manner too, he had an indescribable air of one who knew the world, and who would not have felt abashed at the governor's dinner table or in King William's court, were it possible that his affairs should call him thither. But the only thing about him that could be fixed upon as remarkable was his staff, which bore the likeness of a great black snake, so curiously wrought that it might almost be seen to twist and wriggle itself like a living serpent. This, of course, must have been an ocular deception, assisted by the uncertain light.

"Come, Goodman Brown," cried his fellow-traveller, "this is a dull pace for the beginning of a journey. Take my staff, if you are so soon weary."

"Friend," said the other, exchanging his slow pace for a full stop, "having kept convenant by meeting thee here, it is my purpose now to return whence I came. I have scruples touching the matter thou wot'st of."

"Sayest thou so?" replied he of the serpent, smiling apart. "Let us walk on, nevertheless, reasoning as we go; and if I convince thee not thou shalt turn back. We are but a little way in the forest yet."

"Too far! too far!" exclaimed the goodman, unconsciously resuming his walk. "My father never went into the woods on such an errand, nor his father before him. We have been a race of honest men and good Christians since the days of the martyrs; and shall I be the first of the name of Brown that ever took this path and kept"—

"Such company, thou wouldst say," observed the elder person, interpreting his pause. "Well said, Goodman Brown! I have been as well acquainted with your family as with ever a one among the Puritans; and that's no trifle to say. I helped your grandfather, the constable, when he lashed the Quaker woman so smartly through the streets of Salem; and it was I that brought your father a pitch-pine knot, kindled at my own heart, to set fire to an Indian village, in King Philip's war. They were my good friends, both; and many a pleasant walk have we had along this path, and returned merrily after midnight. I would fain be friends with you for their sake."

"If it be as thou sayest," replied Goodman Brown, "I marvel they never spoke of these matters; or, verily, I marvel not, seeing that the least rumor of the sort would have driven them from New England. We are a people of prayer, and good works to boot, and abide no such wickedness."

"Wickedness or not," said the traveller with the twisted staff, "I have a very general acquaintance here in New England. The deacons of many a church have drunk the communion wine with me; the selectmen of divers towns make me their chairman; and a majority of the Great and General court are firm supporters of my interest. The governor and I, too—But these are state secrets."

"Can this be so?" cried Goodman Brown, with a stare of amazement at his undisturbed companion. "Howbeit, I have nothing to do with the governor and council; they have their own ways, and are no rule for a simple husbandman like me. But, were I to go on with thee, how should I meet the eye of that good old man, our minister, at Salem village? Oh, his voice would make me tremble both Sabbath day and lecture day."

Thus far the elder traveller had listened with due gravity; but now burst into a fit of irrepressible mirth, shaking himself so violently that his snake-like staff actually seemed to wriggle in sympathy.

"Ha! ha! ha!" shouted he again and again; then composing himself, "Well, go on, Goodman Brown, go on; but, prithee, don't kill me with laughing."

"Well, then, to end the matter at once," said Goodman Brown, considerably nettled, "there is my wife, Faith. It would break her dear little heart; and I'd rather break my own."

"Nay, if that be the case," answered the other, "e'en go thy ways, Goodman Brown, I would not for twenty old women like the one hobbling before us that Faith should come to any harm."

As he spoke he pointed his staff at a female figure on the path, in whom Goodman Brown recognized a very pious and exemplary dame, who had taught him his catechism in youth, and was still his moral and spiritual adviser, jointly with the minister and Deacon Gookin.

"A marvel, truly, that Goody Cloyse should be so far in the wilderness at nightfall," said he. "But with your leave, friend, I shall take a cut through the woods until we have left this Christian woman behind. Being a stranger to you, she might ask whom I was consorting with and whither I was going."

"Be it so," said his fellow-traveller. "Betake you to the woods, and let me keep the path."

Accordingly the young man turned aside, but took care to watch his companion, who advanced softly along the road until he had come within a staff's length of the old dame. She, meanwhile, was making the best of her way, with singular speed for so aged a woman, and mumbling some indistinct words—a prayer, doubtless—as she went. The traveller put forth his staff and touched her withered neck with what seemed the serpent's tail.

"The devil!" screamed the pious old lady.

"Then Goody Cloyse knows her old friend?" observed the traveller, confronting her and leaning on his writhing stick.

"Ah, forsooth, and is it your worship indeed?" cried the good dame. "Yea, truly is it, and in the very image of my old gossip, Goodman Brown, the grandfather of the silly fellow that now is. But—would your worship believe it?—my broomstick hath strangely disappeared, stolen, as I suspect, by that unhanged witch, Goody Cory, and that, too, when I was all anointed with the juice of small-age, and cinquefoil, and wolf's bane"—

"Mingled with fine wheat and the fat of a new-born babe," said the shape of old Goodman Brown.

"Ah, your worship knows the recipe," cried the old lady, cackling aloud. "So, as I was saying, being all ready for the meeting, and no horse to ride on, I made up my mind to foot it; for they tell me there is a nice young man to be taken into communion to-night. But now your good worship will lend me your arm, and we shall be there in a twinkling."

"That can hardly be," answered her friend. "I may not spare you my arm, Goody Cloyse; but here is my staff, if you will."

So saying, he threw it down at her feet, where, perhaps, it assumed life, being one of the rods which its owner had formerly lent to the Egyptian magi. Of this fact, however, Goodman Brown could not take cognizance. He had cast up his eyes in astonishment, and, looking down again, beheld neither Goody Cloyse nor the serpentine staff, but his fellow-traveller alone, who waited for him as calmly as if nothing had happened.

"That old woman taught me my catechism," said the young man; and there was a world of meaning in this simple comment.

They continued to walk onward, while the elder traveller exhorted his companion to make good speed and persevere in the path, discoursing so aptly that his arguments seemed rather to spring up in the bosom of his auditor than to be suggested by himself. As they went, he plucked a branch of maple to serve for a walking stick, and began to strip it of the twigs and little boughs, which were wet with evening dew. The moment his fingers touched them they became strangely withered and dried up as with a week's sunshine. Thus the pair proceeded, at a good free pace, until suddenly, in a gloomy hollow of the road, Goodman Brown sat himself down on the stump of a tree and refused to go any farther.

"Friend," said he, stubbornly, "my mind is made up. Not another step will I budge on this errand. What if a wretched old woman do choose to go to the devil when I thought she was going to heaven: is that any reason why I should quit my dear Faith and go after her?"

"You will think better of this by and by," said his acquaintance, composedly, "Sit here and rest yourself a while; and when you feel like moving again, there is my staff to help you along."

Without more words, he threw his companion the maple stick, and was as speedily out of sight as if he had vanished into the deepening gloom. The young man sat a few moments by the roadside, applauding himself greatly, and thinking with how clear a conscience he should meet the minister in his morning walk, nor shrink from the eye of good old Deacon Gookin. And what calm sleep would be his that very night, which was to have been spent so wickedly, but so purely and sweetly now, in the arms of Faith! Amidst these pleasant and praiseworthy meditations, Goodman Brown heard the tramp of horses along the road, and deemed it advisable to conceal himself within the verge of the forest, conscious of the guilty purpose that had brought him thither, though now so happily turned from it.

On came the hoof tramps and the voices of the riders, two grave old voices, conversing soberly as they drew near. These mingled sounds appeared to pass along the road, within a few yards of the young man's hiding-place; but, owing doubtless to the depth of the gloom at that particular spot, neither the travellers nor their steeds were visible. Though their figures brushed the small boughs by the wayside, it could not be seen that they intercepted, even for a moment, the faint gleam from the strip of bright sky athwart which they must have passed. Goodman Brown alternately crouched and stood on tiptoe, pulling aside the branches and thrusting forth his head as far as he durst without discerning so much as a shadow. It vexed him the more, because he could have sworn, were such a thing possible, that he recognized the voices of the minister and Deacon Gookin, jogging along quietly, as they were wont to do, when bound to some ordination or ecclesiastical council. While yet within hearing, one of the riders stopped to pluck a switch.

"Of the two, reverend sir," said the voice like the deacon's, "I had rather miss an ordination dinner than to-night's meeting. They tell me that some of our community are to be here from Falmouth and beyond, and others from Connecticut and Rhode Island, besides several of the Indian powwows, who, after their fashion, know almost as much dev-iltry as the best of us. Moreover, there is a goodly young woman to be taken into communion."

"Mighty well, Deacon Gookin!" replied the solemn old tones of the minister. "Spur up, or we shall be late. Nothing can be done, you know, until I get on the ground."

The hoofs clattered again; and the voices, talking so strangely in the empty air, passed on through the forest, where no church had ever been gathered or solitary Christian prayed. Whither, then, could these holy men be journeying so deep into the heathen wilderness? Young Good-man Brown caught hold of a tree for support, being ready to sink down on the ground, faint and overburdened with the heavy sickness of his heart. He looked up to the sky, doubting whether there really was a heaven above him. Yet there was the blue arch, and the stars bright-ening in it.

"With heaven above and Faith below, I will yet stand firm against the devil!" cried Goodman Brown.

While he still gazed upward into the deep arch of the firmament and had lifted his hands to pray, a cloud, though no wind was stirring, hurried across the zenith and hid the brightening stars. The blue sky was still visible, except directly overhead, where this black mass of cloud was sweeping swiftly northward. Aloft in the air, as if from the depths of the cloud, came a confused and doubtful sound of voices. Once the listener fancied that he could distinguish the accents of towns-people of his own, men and women, both pious and ungodly, many of whom he had met at the communion table, and had seen others rioting at the tavern. The next moment, so indistinct were the sounds, he doubted whether he had heard aught but the murmur of the old forest, whispering without a wind. Then came a stronger swell of those familiar tones, heard daily in the sunshine at Salem village, but never until now from a cloud of night. There was one voice, of a young woman, uttering lamentations, yet with an uncertain sorrow, and entreating for some favor, which, perhaps, it would grieve her to obtain; and all the unseen multitude, both saints and sinners, seemed to encourage her onward.

"Faith!" shouted Goodman Brown, in a voice of agony and desperation; and the echoes of the forest mocked him, crying, "Faith! Faith!" as if bewildered wretches were seeking her all through the wilderness.

The cry of grief, rage, and terror was yet piercing the night, when the unhappy husband held his breath for a response. There was a scream, drowned immediately in a louder murmur of voices, fading into far-off laughter, as the dark cloud swept away, leaving the clear and silent sky above Goodman Brown. But something fluttered lightly down through the air and caught on the branch of a tree. The young man seized it, and beheld a pink ribbon.

"My Faith is gone!" cried he, after one stupefied moment. "There is no good on earth; and sin is but a name. Come, devil; for to thee is this world given."

And, maddened with despair, so that he laughed loud and long, did Goodman Brown grasp his staff and set forth again, at such a rate that he seemed to fly along the forest path rather than to walk or run. The road grew wilder and drearier and more faintly traced, and vanished at length, leaving him in the heart of the dark wilderness, still rushing onward with the instinct that guides mortal man to evil. The whole forest was peopled with frightful sounds—the creaking of the trees, the howling of wild beasts, and the yell of Indians; while sometimes the wind tolled like a distant church bell, and sometimes gave a broad roar around the traveller, as if all Nature were laughing him to scorn. But he was himself the chief horror of the scene, and shrank not from its other horrors.

"Ha! ha! ha!" roared Goodman Brown when the wind laughed at him. "Let us hear which will laugh loudest. Think not to frighten me with your deviltry. Come witch, come wizard, come Indian powwow, come devil himself, and here comes Goodman Brown. You may as well fear him as he fear you."

In truth, all through the haunted forest there could be nothing more frightful than the figure of Goodman Brown. On he flew among the black pines, brandishing his staff with frenzied gestures, now giving vent to an inspiration of horrid blasphemy, and now shouting forth such laughter as set all the echoes of the forest laughing like demons around him. The fiend in his own shape is less hideous than when he rages in the breast of man. Thus sped the demoniac on his course, until, quivering among the trees, he saw a red light before him, as when the felled trunks and branches of a clearing have been set on fire, and throw up their lurid blaze against the sky, at the hour of midnight. He paused, in a lull of the tempest that had driven him onward, and heard the swell of what seemed a hymn, rolling solemnly from a distance with the weight of many voices. He knew the tune; it was a familiar one in the choir of the village meeting-house. The verse died heavily away, and was lengthened by a chorus, not of human voices, but of all the sounds of the benighted wilderness pealing in awful harmony together. Goodman Brown cried out, and his cry was lost to his own ear by its unison with the cry of the desert.

In the interval of silence he stole forward until the light glared full upon his eyes. At one extremity of an open space, hemmed in by the dark wall of forest, arose a rock, bearing some rude, natural resemblance either to an altar or a pulpit, and surrounded by four blazing pines, their tops aflame, their stems untouched, like candles at an evening meeting. The mass of foliage that had overgrown the summit of the rock was all on fire, blazing high into the night and fitfully illuminating the whole field. Each pendent twig and leafy festoon was in a blaze. As the red light arose and fell, a numerous congregation alternately shone forth, then disappeared in shadow, and again grew, as it were, out of the darkness, peopling the heart of the solitary woods at once.

"A grave and dark-clad company," quoth Goodman Brown.

In truth they were such. Among them, quivering to and fro between gloom and splendor, appeared faces that would be seen next day at the council board of the province, and others which, Sabbath after Sabbath, looked devoutly heavenward, and benignantly over the crowded pews, from the holiest pulpits in the land. Some affirm that the lady of the governor was there. At least there were high dames well known to her, and wives of honored husbands, and widows, a great multitude, and ancient maidens, all of excellent repute, and fair young girls, who trembled lest their mothers should espy them. Either the sudden gleams of light flashing over the obscure field bedazzled Goodman Brown, or he recognized a score of the church members of Salem village famous for their especial sanctity. Good old Deacon Gookin had arrived, and waited at the skirts of that venerable saint, his revered pastor. But, irreverently consorting with these grave, reputable, and pious people, these elders of the church, these chaste dames and dewy virgins, there were men of dissolute lives and women of spotted fame, wretches given over to all mean and filthy vice, and suspected even of horrid crimes. It was strange to see that the good shrank not from the wicked, nor were the sinners abashed by the saints. Scattered also among their pale-faced enemies were the Indian priests, or powwows, who had often scared their native forest with more hideous incantations than any known to English witchcraft.

"But where is Faith?" thought Goodman Brown; and, as hope came into his heart, he trembled.

Another verse of the hymn arose, a slow and mournful strain, such as the pious love, but joined to words which expressed all that our nature can conceive of sin, and darkly hinted at far more. Unfathomable to mere mortals is the lore of fiends. Verse after verse was sung; and still the chorus of the desert swelled between like the deepest tone of a mighty organ; and with the final peal of that dreadful anthem there came a sound, as if the roaring wind, the rushing streams, the howling beasts, and every other voice of the unconcerted wilderness were mingling and according with the voice of guilty man in homage to the prince of all. The four blazing pines threw up a loftier flame, and obscurely discovered shapes and visages of horror on the smoke wreaths above the impious assembly. At the same moment the fire on the rock shot redly forth and formed a glowing arch above its base, where now appeared a figure. With reverence be it spoken, the figure bore no slight similitude, both in garb and manner, to some grave divine of the New England churches.

"Bring forth the converts!" cried a voice that echoed through the field and rolled into the forest.

At the word, Goodman Brown stepped forth from the shadow of the trees and approached the congregation, with whom he felt a loathful brotherhood by the sympathy of all that was wicked in his heart. He could have well-nigh sworn that the shape of his own dead father beckoned him to advance, looking downward from a smoke wreath, while a woman, with dim features of despair, threw out her hand to warn him back. Was it his mother? But he had no power to retreat one step, nor to resist, even in thought, when the minister and good old Deacon Gookin seized his arms and led him to the blazing rock. Thither came also the slender form of a veiled female, led between Goody Cloyse, that pious teacher of the catechism, and Martha Carrier, who had received the devil's promise to be queen of hell. A rampant hag was she. And there stood the proselytes beneath the canopy of fire.

"Welcome, my children," said the dark figure, "to the communion of your race. Ye have found thus young your nature and your destiny. My children, look behind you!"

They turned; and flashing forth, as it were, in a sheet of flame, the fiend worshippers were seen; the smile of welcome gleamed darkly on every visage.

"There," resumed the sable form, "are all whom ye have reverenced from youth. Ye deemed them holier than yourselves and shrank from your own sin, contrasting it with their lives of righteousness and prayerful aspirations heavenward. Yet here are they all in my worshipping assembly. This night it shall be granted you to know their secret deeds: how hoary-bearded elders of the church have whispered wanton words to the young maids of their households; how many a woman, eager for widows' weeds, has given her husband a drink at bedtime and let him sleep his last sleep in her bosom; how beardless youths have made haste to inherit their fathers' wealth; and how fair damsels—blush not, sweet ones—have dug little graves in the garden, and bidden me, the sole guest, to an infant's funeral. By the sympathy of your human hearts for sin ye shall scent out all the places—whether in church, bedchamber, street, field, or forest—where crime has been committed, and shall exult to behold the whole earth one stain of guilt, one mighty blood spot. Far more than this. It shall be yours to penetrate, in every bosom, the deep mystery of sin, the fountain of all wicked arts, and which inexhaustibly supplies more evil impulses than human power—than my power at its utmost—can make manifest in deeds. And now, my children, look upon each other."

They did so; and, by the blaze of the hell-kindled torches, the wretched man beheld his Faith, and the wife her husband, trembling before that unhallowed altar.

"Lo, there ye stand, my children," said the figure, in a deep and solemn tone, almost sad with its despairing awfulness, as if his once angelic nature could yet mourn for our miserable race. "Depending upon one another's hearts, ye had still hoped that virtue were not all a dream. Now are ye undeceived. Evil is the nature of mankind. Evil must be your only happiness. Welcome again, my children, to the communion of your race."

"Welcome," repeated the fiend worshippers, in one cry of despair and triumph.

And there they stood, the only pair, as it seemed, who were yet hesitating on the verge of wickedness in this dark world. A basin was hollowed, naturally, in the rock. Did it contain water, reddened by the lurid light? or was it blood? or, perchance, a liquid flame? Herein did the shape of evil dip his hand and prepare to lay the mark of baptism upon their foreheads, that they might be partakers of the mystery of sin, more conscious of the secret guilt of others, both in deed and thought, than they could now be of their own. The husband cast one look at his pale wife, and Faith at him. What polluted wretches would the next glance show them to each other, shuddering alike at what they disclosed and what they saw!

"Faith! Faith!" cried the husband, "look up to heaven, and resist the wicked one."

Whether Faith obeyed he knew not. Hardly had he spoken when he found himself amid calm night and solitude, listening to a roar of the wind which died heavily away through the forest. He staggered against the rock, and felt it chill and damp; while a hanging twig, that had been all on fire, besprinkled his cheek with the coldest dew.

The next morning young Goodman Brown came slowly into the street of Salem village, staring around him like a bewildered man. The good old minister was taking a walk along the graveyard to get an appetite for breakfast and meditate his sermon, and bestowed a blessing, as he passed, on Goodman Brown. He shrank from the venerable saint as if to avoid an anathema. Old Deacon Gookin was at domestic worship, and the holy words of his prayer were heard through the open window. "What God doth the wizard pray to?" quoth Goodman Brown. Goody Cloyse, that excellent old Christian, stood in the early sunshine at her own lattice, catechizing a little girl who had brought her a pint of morning's milk. Goodman Brown snatched away the child as from the grasp of the fiend himself. Turning the corner by the meeting-house, he spied the head of Faith, with the pink ribbons, gazing anxiously forth, and bursting into such joy at sight of him that she skipped along the street and almost kissed her husband before the whole village. But Goodman Brown looked sternly and sadly into her face, and passed on without a greeting.

Had Goodman Brown fallen asleep in the forest and only dreamed a wild dream of a witch-meeting?

Be it so if you will; but alas! it was a dream of evil omen for young Goodman Brown. A stern, a sad, a darkly meditative, a distrustful, if not a desperate man did he become from the night of that fearful dream. On the Sabbath day, when the congregation were singing a holy psalm, he could not listen because an anthem of sin rushed loudly upon his ear and drowned all the blessed strain. When the minister spoke from the pulpit with power and fervid eloquence, and, with his hand on the open Bible, of the sacred truths of our religion, and of saint-like lives and triumphant deaths, and of future bliss or misery unutterable, then did Goodman Brown turn pale, dreading lest the roof should thunder down upon the gray blasphemer and his hearers. Often, awaking suddenly at midnight, he shrank from the bosom of Faith; and at morning or eventide, when the family knelt down at prayer, he scowled and muttered to himself, and gazed sternly at his wife, and turned away. And when he had lived long, and was borne to his grave a hoary corpse, followed by Faith, an aged woman, and children and grandchildren, a goodly procession, besides neighbors not a few, they carved no hopeful verse upon his tombstone, for his dying hour was gloom.

1835

FOR FURTHER READING

As I mentioned in the text, in the last twenty years, we've seen an explosion of critical studies of fiction. What appears below can only claim to indicate some of the most important and influential works on the subject.

Allen, Walter. *The English Novel: A Short Critical History*. New York: Dutton, 1954. More than thirty years after publication, still a valuable one-volume survey.

Bakhtin, M. M. *The Dialogic Imagination*. Austin, TX: University of Texas, 1981.

—— *Problems of Dostoevsky's Poetics*. Minneapolis, MN: University of Minnesota, 1984.

—— *Rabelais and His World*. Bloomington, IN: University of Indiana, 1984. In the last few years, Bakhtin has emerged as one of the major influences on serious contemporary criticism of fiction. Though some readers may find his work difficult at first reading, it is ultimately rewarding.

Barthes, Roland. *Image-Music-Text*. New York: Hill and Wang, 1977. See pp. 79–124 for a rigorous treatment of narrative. Difficult.

Booth, Wayne C. *The Rhetoric of Fiction*. Chicago: University of Chicago, 1961. One of the classics in the field. Discussions of "implied author," "unreliable narrator," etc. Just about anyone—at least in the English-speaking world—who writes about fiction has been influenced by this work.

Brooks, Peter. *Reading for the Plot*. New York: Knopf, 1984. On plot as central to structure and meaning in fiction.

Burke, Kenneth. *Counter-Statement*. Berkeley, CA: University of California, 1968. "Lexicon Rhetoricae" and "Psychology and Form" are especially relevant to issues discussed here.

Chatman, Seymour. *Story and Discourse*. Ithaca, NY: Cornell, 1978. Makes accessible much of the current thought on fiction.

Cohn, Dorrit. *Transparent Minds*. Princeton, NJ: Princeton University, 1978. On the presentation of consciousness in fiction; sophisticated treatment of issues related to point of view.

Forster, E. M. *Aspects of the Novel*. New York: Harcourt Brace Jovanovich, 1927. Still relevant; discussion of story and plot and of "flat" and "round" characters have been widely influential. And, as one would expect from this author, beautifully written.

Iser, Wolfgang. *The Act of Reading.* Baltimore: Johns Hopkins, 1976.

——— *The Implied Reader.* Baltimore: Johns Hopkins, 1974. Of the two important studies by Wolfgang Iser of the reader's reception of fiction, this one is the more accessible.

Leitch, Thomas. *What Stories Are.* University Park, PA: Pennsylvania State University, 1986. An excellent recent study with some particularly provocative comments on plot.

Lodge, David. *Language of Fiction.* New York: Columbia, 1966. Emphasis on style as an element of fiction.

Lukacs, Georg. *The Historical Novel.* Lincoln, NE: University of Nebraska, 1983.

——— *Theory of the Novel.* Cambridge, MA: MIT Press, 1973. This and *The Historical Novel* by Lukacs are two important works by one of the great critics of fiction and one of the great champions of realism.

Martin, Wallace. *Recent Theories of Narrative.* Ithaca, NY: Cornell, 1986. Excellent guide to recent developments; concerned with narrative in general, but obviously of interest to the student of fiction.

Pavel, Thomas. *Fictional Worlds.* Cambridge, MA: Harvard, 1986. Sophisticated study of representation in fiction.

Rabinowitz, Peter J. *Before Reading.* Ithaca, NY: Cornell, 1987. Readable, often witty study of conventions readers bring to the act of reading.

Rimmon-Kenan, Shlomith. *Narrative Fiction: Contemporary Poetics.* New York: Methuen, 1983. Systematic treatment of the question of what makes narrative fiction narrative fiction; concise and informed.

Scholes, Robert, and Robert Kellogg. *The Nature of Narrative.* New York: Oxford, 1968. Illuminating on varieties of narrative and on their interaction.

Stanzel, F. K. *A Theory of Narrative.* Cambridge: Cambridge University, 1984. Systematic treatment of point of view.

Suleiman, Susan, and Inge Crosman, eds. *The Reader in the Text.* Princeton, NJ: Princeton University, 1980. An anthology of essays reflecting the pragmatic approach, many of them focusing on fiction.

Uspensky, Boris. *A Poetics of Composition*. Berkeley, CA: University of California, 1983. One of the most brilliant studies on point of view.

Watt, Ian. *The Rise of the Novel*. Berkeley, CA: University of California, 1959. A study of the early development of the novel that casts light on the nature of the form.

INDEX OF TITLES AND AUTHORS

INDEX OF TOPICS